D0595744

"No mind numbing theo-babble here. *Everyday Epiphanies: Seeing the Sacred in Everything* is a book for those sensitive enough to practice the 'art of small.' Filled with well written reflections, this is a book that will enlarge your soul, helping you see the God of the "Ever" in everydayness. This is a book for those who find themselves between a rock and a hard place and looking for some small wise words that will help ease the pressure of everyday stress."

John Powers, C.P.
Author, *Seeking Inner Peace: The Art of Facing Your Emotions*

"Sr. Melannie once again displays her unique ability to provide profound spiritual wisdom in a graphic and delightful manner. The arrangement of her reflections in reader-friendly brief stories and observations offer rich nourishment in portions suited to busy people."

Rev. Demetrius Dumm, O.S.B.
Saint Vincent Archabbey
Latrobe, PA

"Surprise is always at the heart of epiphany. This is a book of surprises. Sr. Melannie exposes a great variety of her own simple, everyday experiences in the hope that some of them will also catch fire in revelation for her readers. But epiphany also requires in the reader an openness and availability of heart. For readers not put off by the simplicity and brevity of many of these reflections, discovery will surprise and enrich their hearts."

George Aschenbrenner, SJ
Director, Jesuit Spiritual Center
Wernersville, PA

"For Melannie Svoboda, the simplest event, the briefest encounter with neighbor or nature, shimmers with God's immanence and intent. Through these pensées two things happen: She gains our trust with her humbling humor and candor about human needs and failings; then she surprises us into praise at sacred blossoming, as every ordinary thing, to her eyes, becomes 'every bloomin' thing.'"

Susan Lowry Rardin
Fiction Writer

MELANNIE SVOBODA, SND

Everyday Epiphanies

Seeing
the Sacred
in Every
Thing

TWENTY-THIRD PUBLICATIONS

Mystic, CT 06355

Third printing 1999

Twenty-Third Publications
185 Willow Street
P.O. Box 180
Mystic, CT 06355
(860) 536-2611
(800) 321-0411

ISBN 0-89622-730-8
Library of Congress Catalog Card Number 97-60485
Printed in the U.S.A.

DEDICATION

To my brother
John M. Svoboda:
by your goodness, generosity,
wisdom, and strength,
you are for me
an epiphany
of God's faithful love.

ACKNOWLEDGMENTS

Upon completing this book, I am reminded that I did not write it by myself or in isolation. An array of individuals contributed to the writing of this book. I would like to thank a few of them here.

First, I thank my family. It was my mother, Mildred, who, through her love for crossword puzzles, passed on to me her fascination for words. My father, John, a tool-and-die maker and farmer, bequeathed to me his great love for reading. To this day Dad is seldom seen without a book, magazine, or newspaper in his hands. I am also grateful to my sister, Mary Ann Hartman, and my brothers, John and Paul. As a little girl, when I sat on the side porch with the old manual typewriter on my lap, pecking out a story or a letter, my siblings did not make fun of me. On the contrary, they gave me the sense that my love for writing was a wonderful (albeit, a little strange) gift.

Secondly, I wish to thank my religious community, the Sisters of Notre Dame of Chardon, Ohio for encouraging me to write and supporting me in this ministry. I am especially indebted to those individuals (sisters, friends, spiritual directors), who, over the years, have helped me to become more attuned to the many epiphanies in my everyday life. In a particular way I wish to thank the Jesuit community at Loyola House Novitiate in Berkley, Michigan where I have ministered these past four years. I appreciate their continued interest in my writing as well as their unmistakable influence upon it.

And finally, I am grateful to the folks at Twenty-Third Publications—especially Neil Kluepfel, Gwen Costello, and Mary Carol Kendzia—whose encouragement and professional expertise have helped bring this book to birth.

Contents

Introduction   1

✒ Summer ✒

1)	"Thy will be done"	5
2)	The three little kids at McDonald's	5
3)	Making a personal investment in the game of life	6
4)	We know in wholes	7
5)	Fringes will do	7
6)	"Do you love me?"	8
7)	Monosyllabic prayer	9
8)	Quotes on happiness	9
9)	Things in heaven	10
10)	Setting the table	10
11)	Thoughts low and lofty	11
12)	Nicodemus	11
13)	Frequent trips to the mailbox	12
14)	Shooting buckshot	13
15)	Emulating Emily	13
16)	On loving hyenas	14
17)	What Jesus didn't say	14
18)	Mrs. Siena	15
19)	Faith and fun	16
20)	Little Hannah	17
21)	Writing is a lot like praying	17
22)	Quotes on faith	18

23)	Letting someone else run the show	19
24)	A sense of humor	19
25)	Introduction to grief	20
26)	The Bible is not escapist literature	21
27)	Honesty and caring	22
28)	Door prizes	22
29)	Learning obedience through beauty	23
30)	Hobo signs	24
31)	Two kids on a slide	25
32)	Mary's prayer at Cana	26
33)	Midsummer's Day dialogues	27
34)	Dialogue with a herd of cows	28
35)	Dialogue with Grandpa Willow Tree	28
36)	The miracle of flight and life	29
37)	A Hasidic story	30
38)	Only God?	30
39)	Thank God for words	31
40)	Quotes on adversity	32
41)	Jesus did not carry a pocket calendar	33
42)	Accepting talents and limitations	33
43)	Gravity is our friend	34
44)	Sensitivity: the art of the small	35
45)	The pristine ministry of conversation	36
46)	The chaplain at the children's hospital	37
47)	Crowns, hearts, and feet in the Bible	38
48)	The roar of the ordinary	39

❧ Fall ❧

49)	Jesus saves	43
50)	God as Father, Grandma, and Coach	43
51)	Geese are not dumb	44
52)	Wait and see	45
53)	Proverbs	46
54)	George Dawson, 98	46
55)	The anatomy lesson	47
56)	God's good company	48
57)	Solving problems with a harp	48
58)	Writing a book	49
59)	Things I've learned as a teacher	50
60)	Jesus never said, "I told you so!"	51
61)	We know who holds the future	52
62)	Quotes on friendship	52
63)	Heaven is coming home	53
64)	What's wrong with God	54
65)	The popular cow	54
66)	St. Francis of Assisi had a sweet tooth	55
67)	The promise of ultimate victory	56
68)	Temporary friendships	57
69)	Mary pondered	58
70)	Throwing bouquets	59
71)	Playing hide-and-seek with a squirrel	60
72)	Quotes on gratitude	61
73)	When it rains on our picnic	61
74)	On giving scandal	62
75)	"Here I am, God"	63

76) Fallow time   64
77) Keep laughing   65
78) God's circus   66
79) Haste makes sense   66
80) Jealousy and our intrinsic ache for "the more"   67
81) The prodigality of the pear trees   68
82) The little girl with the yellow bow   69
83) Ministry: punishment or privilege?   70
84) Experiencing pleasure   71
85) "Give this matter the attention it deserves"   72
86) Humility and the illusion of
      personal autonomy   73
87) Putting the groceries away   74
88) God likes spunk   75
89) "It's okay to have a crabby day"   76
90) The tyranny of personal preference   77

❧ WINTER ❧

91) "The conviction of things not seen"   81
92) One sentence at a time   81
93) Befriending darkness   82
94) "You are a doe"   83
95) Quotes on wisdom   84
96) The silver chalice: a sacred trust   85
97) The inner child   86
98) Look again   87
99) Gesture as prayer   88

100)	Befriending the older and the younger	89
101)	"Come, Lord Jesus!"	90
102)	The Song of Songs	90
103)	A world without animals	91
104)	Mary as intercessor	92
105)	Button up your overcoat	93
106)	The need to please	94
107)	Humorous observations	95
108)	Criticism: speaking the truth in love	96
109)	Inviting God to take over	97
110)	Working and loafing	98
111)	Emmanuel	99
112)	All was not calm, all was not bright	100
113)	God works through all kinds of people	101
114)	Trying to become a good person	102
115)	Enlarging our borders	102
116)	Fear is a funny thing	103
117)	New Year's resolutions	105
118)	What's in a name?	106
119)	On being perfect	107
120)	St. Valentine's Day	108
121)	Quotes on God	109
122)	I yawned at Mass today	110
123)	Homilies	111
124)	The school crossing guard	112
125)	Will the magic happen again today?	113
126)	Impure thoughts	114
127)	Emperor penguins	115

128) My mother and the vacuum cleaner bags   116
129) Remember to remember   117
130) The good thing about being an addict   119
131) For a God I know and love   120
132) Looking for God in unfamiliar places   121
133) Crossword puzzles   122

⚘ SPRING ⚘

134) The newborn calf   127
135) Conversion   128
136) Offer it up   129
137) Wonder: Behold!   130
138) Quotes on life   131
139) "It's all right"   132
140) Naming things   133
141) Throwing seed with open hands   133
142) A parent's love   134
143) "Like *what?*"   135
144) On aging   136
145) The parable of the brownies   137
146) Silence   138
147) Good prayer   139
148) My football career   140
149) Is order heaven's first law?   141
150) A horse named Lucky   143
151) An alternate perception   144
152) Lent and the process of repenting   144

153) The writing lesson   145
154) Hummingbirds   147
155) Quotes on opportunity   148
156) The beckoning risen Jesus   149
157) Easter surprises   150
158) A religious person   151
159) Funeral plans   152
160) The parable of the Last Judgment   153
161) "I want to want!"   154
162) Quilting: "That's what piecing is"   155
163) Draw what you see   155
164) The deer principle   157
165) Humorous observations about sundry items   158
166) The spirituality of wishing   159
167) It all depends on angle and framing   160
168) Our image of the truth   160
169) Happiness   162
170) On going to bed at night   163
171) Quotes from obscure sources   163
172) Sloth   164
173) Jesus: Prince of Peace or Agitation?   165
174) Taking time for the pain   166
175) Babies: one of God's greatest ideas   167

INDEX   170

Everyday Epiphanies

INTRODUCTION

It happens every day.

You're brushing your teeth in the morning and all of a sudden you get some insight into a problem you've been struggling with for days. Or you're reading a familiar passage from scripture and, without warning, a word or phrase jumps out at you as it never has before. Or you're standing in the checkout line in the grocery store when, for no apparent reason, you suddenly feel very close to God. Or you're sipping a cup of coffee with a friend, and she makes a remark that gives you a brand new way of looking at something.

Call these experiences what you will: moments of insight, inspiration, or grace. I like to call them mini-epiphanies. Strictly speaking, the word epiphany means an appearance or manifestation of God. In scripture, we find many epiphanies. Moses, for example, experienced an epiphany when he encountered God in the burning bush. Later, he had several other epiphanies when he dialogued with God amid thunder and lightning on Mt. Sinai.

Our Christian feast of the Epiphany commemorates other manifestations of God: Christ's manifestation to the Magi as well as his manifestations at his baptism and the wedding feast of Cana. The burning bush, the thunder on Sinai, Christ before the Magi, the miracle at Cana—all are epiphanies, that is, all are dramatic manifestations of God in human lives.

The mini-epiphanies of which I speak here, however, are not that dramatic or earth-shaking. They are more subtle and ordinary. In a word, more everyday. We experience these so-called everyday epiphanies every time we gain a new insight into some aspect of our faith, feel good about a choice we've made, learn a worthwhile lesson from a bad mistake, delight in some simple pleasure, discover some good in an apparently bad situation, find ourselves thanking God for our blessings, or stand in wonder and awe before the unfathomable mystery of existence.

Everyday epiphanies may at first seem insignificant. In fact, they can almost pass unnoticed. Yet they are very real and potent. Charged with power, they can, over time, produce critical changes in our awareness, attitude, and behavior.

This book is a collection of short reflections based on some of the everyday epiphanies in my own life. Although in one sense these are my epiphanies, in another sense they are not; many of them, I'm sure, will resonate with you and your own experience. After all, haven't we all munched on an apple, trekked to the mailbox, struggled with prayer, worried about someone we love, admired a flower, copied down a quote we liked, crawled exhausted into bed at night? The reflections in this book focus on a wide range of topics from anger to zeal, from friendship to loneliness, from saints to sinners, from prayer to popularity. Many are directly rooted in scripture. All conclude with a brief prayer.

Everyday Epiphanies is arranged in four parts: summer, fall, winter, spring. Seasonal reflections can be found under the respective season. Those dealing with Christmas, for example, can be found under winter; those for Lent and Easter, under spring. As I see it, you can read this book in two ways. You can start at the beginning and read the entries in order—one each day, if you wish. Or you can read the book according to topic. Just look up a particular topic in the index—for example, "Jesus," "faith," "humor," "nature"—and read the reflection or reflections on that particular topic. (The numbers in the index refer to the numbers of the reflections, and not the page numbers. Check the Table of Contents to find the page on which a particular reflection is located.)

My hope in writing *Everyday Epiphanies* is simple: that we all might become more sensitive to the many subtle manifestations of God in our everyday lives—those instances when we suddenly feel we have learned a precious lesson, grasped a truth that heretofore had eluded us, brushed up against the holy, or caught a glimpse of the eternal in the here and now.

In summer, I stalk. Summer leaves obscure, heat dazzles, and creatures hide from the red-eyed sun, and me. I have to seek things out.

—*Annie Dillard*

SUMMER

1) "Thy will be done"

The paradigm of prayer is, "Thy will be done." This is in essence what Mary said at the Annunciation: "Let it be done unto me according to your word" (Lk 1:38). This is what Jesus prayed to Abba in the garden of Gethsemane: "Not my will but yours be done" (Lk 22:42). But it is good for us to remember that their prayer did not begin there.

Mary's prayer began in perplexity: "She was greatly troubled" (Lk 1:29). Then it moved into questioning: "How can this be?" (Lk 1:34). Only then did Mary pray "Thy will be done...." Similarly, Jesus began his prayer in Gethsemane by telling God what he wanted and then begging God "to remove this cup" (Lk 22:42). Only then did he pray "Thy will be done."

Like the prayer of Mary and Jesus, our prayer may not always begin with "Thy will be done" either. It too may need to pass through other stages first. When disappointments occur in our lives or something terrifying looms, we may not be able to say immediately to God, "Thy will be done." And that's all right. Our prayer may need to take other forms first, such as sitting in perplexity, asking God questions, and begging God to give us what we see as good.

God, help me to be more accepting of whatever form my prayer takes today.

☞ ☞ ☞

2) The three little kids at McDonald's

The three little kids came into McDonald's with their father. While he carefully placed their order, the kids jumped up and down in eager anticipation of their meal. A few moments later as their father gingerly carried the heaping tray to a table, the children's eyes were fixed on the array of brightly colored boxes, bags, and cups. As the man placed a hamburger and fries before each child, each one responded with an enthusiastic, "Thank you!" One of them, the little girl, even clapped.

I was struck by the children's uninhibited display of joy and excitement—and all over a couple of hamburgers, too! For there I sat, in a booth across from them, calmly consuming my meal, my composure a stark contrast to their exuberance. Obviously, the children hadn't learned yet to conceal their enthusiasm—or at least to subdue it. They hadn't learned yet that showing too much joy and excitement is not "cool."

I wondered: at what age do we start acting cool? And (for heaven's sake!) why?

God, restore my ability to show joy and enthusiasm.

∂ ∂ ∂

3) Making a personal investment in the game of life

To watch a baseball or football game without taking sides may be very relaxing, but it offers little challenge, excitement, or fun. I prefer to be for one of the two teams—either as a player or a coach or (at least) a diehard fan. In whatever way I can, I want to make a personal contribution to the game, a personal investment in its outcome—by my playing, my coaching, or my cheers.

The same is true of the more important contests in life—especially the primordial conflict between good and evil that is being played out before us right now on the fields of human history. I can't ignore this conflict. I can't just sit by and watch others struggling. I myself must become personally involved in that contest. I must make some kind of an investment in the outcome of that struggle—whether directly by my actions or indirectly by my counsel and prayers.

That's precisely what it means to be a Christian. It means taking sides—the side of the good. It means being on Jesus' team. It means making a personal investment toward the outcome of human history with the whole of our lives.

Jesus, enable me to make a personal investment on the side of the good today.

4) We know in wholes

We know in wholes, but we realize in bits and pieces. We all know, for example, that we are going to die. But we realize it only gradually, step by step, inch by inch. Perhaps we're in a near fatal accident. Or maybe we're suddenly faced with a serious illness. Or one day we wake up with a kink in our lower back. Only then do we realize in part what we already know in full: we are mortal. We are going to die.

Realization arrives late at life's party, only to discover that knowledge has been there the whole time.

God, help me to realize today what I already know.

5) Fringes will do

During Mass today, I feel as if I'm standing on the outskirts of the church, the fringes of the congregation. I feel as if all the other people in the church are really present and fully attentive to what's going on at the altar, whereas I am only partly there, hovering at a distance. I don't like feeling this way. I want to feel completely at one with the sacred mystery. At dead center, so to speak.

My consolation every time this happens? The story of the woman with the hemorrhage (Lk 8:43–48). Her aim was simple enough: to touch but the tassels of Jesus' garment, the fringes, if you will. She told herself, "Touching them will be enough to heal me." So she did, and instantly, the woman was cured of her debilitating and embarrassing infirmity.

On days like today, this nameless woman reminds me of this great truth: when it comes to touching the holy—whether through liturgy or prayer or loving—fringes will do. For even the tassels of God's garment have the power to heal us of all our infirmities.

God, make me more aware of the ways today I will touch your fringes.

6) "Do you love me?"

"Do you love me?" This is the question Jesus asks Peter on the shore of the sea of Galilee after Jesus' resurrection, and (more significantly) after Peter's betrayal (Jn 21:15). Jesus does not ask Peter:

"Do you know how to run a church?"

"Can you write a good encyclical?"

"How good are you at fundraising?"

No. Jesus asks, "Do you love me?" And if the disciple's answer to that question is "yes," then all the other things will fall into their proper place. If the answer is "no," however, the other things don't matter at all.

Jesus, may I always answer your question "Do you love me?" with a resounding YES!

7) Monosyllabic prayer

Sometimes our best prayer is monosyllabic: "Jesus!" or "Help!" or "Why?" In the traditional English translation of the Our Father, there are only fifty-six words. And forty of them are monosyllabic: our...be thy name...will be done on earth...give us this day...bread...lead us not.

Maybe Jesus was trying to tell us something. When it comes to finding the right words in prayer, shorter is good, fewer is better. And don't all the great mystics of the church tell us this: no words can be the best prayer of all?

God, help me to pray with few and short words today—or maybe with no words at all.

8) Quotes on happiness

Happiness is not a goal; it is a by-product. (Eleanor Roosevelt)

Happiness is not mostly pleasure; it is mostly victory. (Harry Emerson Fosdick)

No one truly knows happiness who has not suffered, and the redeemed are happier than the elect. (Henri Amiel)

Happiness is an inside job. (William Arthur Ward)

If you want others to be happy, practice compassion. If you want to be happy, practice compassion. (Dalai Lama)

God, show me how I can practice compassion today.

9) Things in heaven

A list of things we probably will not find in heaven:
locks...clocks...handcuffs...scales...aspirin...erasers...parking meters..."for sale" signs...insurance policies...hearses...handkerchiefs...

God, give me a greater appreciation of heaven.

10) Setting the table

She did not set or decorate the table for supper. It was a feastday and we were expecting guests. It was her responsibility, and she said she would do it. Angrily, I stomped over to the cupboard, jerked open a drawer, and grabbed a clean tablecloth. Stomping back to the table, I yanked off the dirty tablecloth, my hasty movements betraying my severe annoyance.

Suddenly I stopped. "Is this any way to set a table—and for guests?" I asked myself. "Is this any way to decorate for a party—in haste and in anger?" Then I heard myself say, "A gift given in such a way is surely no gift at all."

Immediately, I closed my eyes and took a few deep breaths. Then I resumed the task set before me—only now I went about my work with calm and care. By the time I finished setting the table, I was humming.

My conclusions: 1) we cannot fashion beauty in haste and anger; 2) gifts are best bestowed with humming.

God, help me to hum as I gently bestow my gifts today.

11) Thoughts low and lofty

It surprises me how easily my low thoughts can coexist with my lofty thoughts. Thoughts such as: "Drop dead!" "I'm sick and tired of being good!" "Get away from me!" "I'm as jealous as hell!" "I hate God!" live side by side with: "I love you!" "I want to be better!" "Can I help?" "I'm really sorry!" "How good God is!"

You'd think the low thoughts would drive out the lofty ones— or vice versa. But no. My low, selfish, mean, petty thoughts share the same house with my lofty, pure, high, noble thoughts.

As Christians, we will probably never rid ourselves completely of those low thoughts that barge into our house uninvited. I suppose, in the long run, our only hope is to welcome and entertain more lofty thoughts than low ones. But there's a certain wisdom (not to mention humility!) in realizing that, at any moment, we are capable of either.

God, help me to entertain lofty thoughts today, but not be shocked if a few low thoughts barge in uninvited.

ᗧ   ᗧ   ᗧ

12) Nicodemus

We are free to come to Jesus at any time: morning, noon, or night. But some of us, like Nicodemus, prefer to come at night (Jn 3:1–21). At night, when no one else can see us. At night, when everything is shrouded in darkness and we have lost our way. At night, when we can see nothing except the face of the Lord illumined by a tiny flicker of faith.

It would be bolder, no doubt, and certainly more dignified and self-satisfying, to approach the Lord in broad daylight—in full view of others, when the road is clearly marked, and when our faith shines as bright as the sun.

But Jesus overlooks our cowardice and desperation. Jesus sees only our coming.

Jesus, no matter what time of day it is in my life, I want to say, "Lord, I'm coming!"

ᘒ ᘒ ᘒ

13) Frequent trips to the mailbox

Being far away from home for any length of time can rattle your self-confidence. You get this awful feeling that the farther and longer you're away, the more the people back home aren't missing you. And you fear they are realizing you aren't as important to them as you or they once thought you were. In fact, your family and friends are getting along quite well without you, thank you, and the unique space you thought you once occupied in their lives is now being filled with other people and other interests.

You begin to think you mean nothing to them—or to anyone else for that matter—and you start doubting your essential worth. That doubting, which used to be little more than a passing fancy, now becomes agonizing certitude.

Little wonder you try to stay back this awful feeling of insignificance by sending postcards and letters—a gesture meant more to remind others of your existence than it is to let them know you're remembering theirs. Every postcard, every letter you send is your way of proclaiming, "Look! It's me! I'm still alive! And I'm remembering you! Are you remembering me?" And your frequent trips to the mailbox (sometimes several times a day!) are a source of embarrassment to yourself—one more incontrovertible sign of your innate insecurity and your desperate need to feel remembered.

Your only consolation? You notice a lot of other people making frequent trips to their mailboxes, too!

I need to feel remembered, God.

14) Shooting buckshot

She cornered me in the hall to share her anger with me. She is furious with several individuals and she just wanted me to know, that's all. Her words came fast and hard—like buckshot—flying in all directions, indiscriminately hitting dozens of people. She eventually set her sights on one person in particular, and blasted away.

I finally said, "Maybe you have to talk to her about that."

"Never!" she shot back. "You can't talk to that woman about anything! She listens to no one!"

Ironically, those are the exact words others have said about her!

Moral: if you shoot enough buckshot, sooner or later you'll end up shooting yourself!

God, I'm sorry if I've shot any buckshot lately.

15) Emulating Emily

Emily Dickinson is a poet of immense giftedness. During her life, she generated hundreds of poems, unique in form, profound in content. Her life is almost as intriguing as her poetry. Emily, by age forty, was something of a recluse. Never married, though rumored to have been in love twice, she seldom left her small house in Amherst.

Emily reminds us that we do not have to travel extensively to grow in knowledge. We do not have to journey far to enjoy rich experiences or gain wisdom. Knowledge sits in our own backyard. Experience awaits us at our kitchen table. Wisdom is as near as our fingertips.

Jesus, too, lived a life that some would call confined. The Son of God was content to live his entire life within the radius of a relatively few miles. Yet who would deny his expanse of knowledge, his range of experience, his depth of wisdom?

If life denies us expansiveness, then let us opt for depth. For every roadblock in one direction can be the impetus for growth in another.

God, give me the wisdom to see how each confinement in my life can be an impetus for growth.

∅ ∅ ∅

16) On loving hyenas

I watched a National Geographic TV show on hyenas featuring a scientist who has studied hyenas for over seven years. Through his intensive research, this man has proven false many of the canards about hyenas. The narrator said of this scientist, "He's probably the only human being on earth who publicly admits, 'I love hyenas.'"

This scientist confirms two theories of mine: 1) If we study anything long enough we are bound to see goodness and beauty where we previously thought none existed. 2) All loving begins with taking the time to better know someone (or some thing!).

God, help me to take time today to know someone better.

∅ ∅ ∅

17) What Jesus didn't say

"What a bunch of mangy fishermen! No potential for leadership there, that's for sure!" (Mt 4:18–22)

"How many times must you forgive? Once seems more than enough to me." (Mt 18:22)

"A funeral? Back there in Nain? No, I didn't notice." (Lk 7:11–15)

"Me? Time for prayer? With all my responsibilities?" (Mk 1:35)

"Thanks, guys, for getting rid of those little brats. I don't have much use for kids." (Lk 18:15–17)

"Lady, take your alabaster jar and get out of here. You're embarrassing me! And put your veil back on your head, for heaven's sake!" (Mk 1:35)

"Give to Caesar what belongs to Caesar—and that's just about everything!" (Mt 22:15–22)

"Psst, Judas! I'm sure we can cut a deal." (Jn 13:21–27)

Jesus, let me hear what you really said in the gospels—and what you are really saying to me today.

∞ ∞ ∞

18) Mrs. Siena

Not all saints got along with their mothers. St. Catherine of Siena, for example, was often at odds with her mother, Lapa. As one biographer put it, "Lapa loved Catherine dearly but understood her not at all."

Lapa was, by any standards, an extraordinary woman. She gave birth to twenty-five children (yes, twenty-five!) of which Catherine was the youngest. The teen years were especially strained for both mother and daughter. Lapa was always nagging Catherine to pay more attention to her appearance so she might snare a well-to-do husband. But Catherine had other ambitions, namely, to be a nun.

One day, when the fifteen year old Catherine was feeling particularly ascetical, she chopped off most of her beautiful golden-brown hair. To conceal the deed from her mother, she donned a small white cap. Suspicious, Lapa snatched off the cap and shrieked in horror, "What have you done?! How could you do this to me?!"

Lapa and Catherine. Their story is a consoling one for any of us who find ourselves at odds with those we love. Living together can be stressful—even for saints!

God, help me to be more patient today with those I love and live with.

☙ ☙ ☙

19) Faith and fun

Mitch Finley, the author of *The Joy of Being Catholic*, has created a new award called the "Grim Catholic Award." According to Finley, he will give the award to "a prominent Catholic who best exemplifies the direct opposite of the joy and tolerance Jesus lived and taught." Finley created the award because he believes strongly that one of God's primary messages to us today is, "Hey, people! Lighten up!"

Sometimes we Christians do tend to get too grim about life. We are quick to say, for example, that the strength of our faith is measured by our ability to suffer. After all, Jesus did say, "Whoever does not carry the cross and follow me cannot be my disciple" (Lk 14:27). But, if we think about it, our ability to suffer is only half the measure of our faith's strength. The other half is our ability to enjoy. For do not all of the Beatitudes begin with the word happy?

Similarly, the Talmud says that a person will be called to account on judgment day for every permissible thing he or she might have enjoyed, but did not. Interesting concept: God actually wants us to enjoy things! God wants us to have fun!

Our faith, if genuine, should constantly be increasing our capacity to enjoy—that is, to appreciate, to laugh, to play, to relish, to delight in, to have a really good time. At the end of each day, our examination of conscience should include a question like this: "How much fun did I have today?"

God, increase my ability to enjoy and my capacity to have fun.

20) Little Hannah

Little Hannah is four years old. Her brother, Aaron, is two. I notice Aaron's shoe is untied. "Come here, Aaron, and let me tie your shoe," I say. He comes to me and I bend down and tie the shoe while Hannah watches closely.

A few minutes later, Hannah comes to me with her pink sandal strap undone. "Do my shoe," she says, sticking her little foot out in front of me. I bend down and buckle the strap, smiling, for I know Hannah herself undid the strap so I would give her the same attention I had given Aaron.

We are all little Hannahs. We are all craving attention—from one another and (more importantly) from God. If only we would realize, when it comes to getting attention from God, the attention is there for the asking. All we have to do is to stick out our unbuckled sandal and say, "Do my shoe—please?"

God, I set before you all that is "unbuckled" in my life.

∽ ∽ ∽

21) Writing is a lot like praying

Writing is a lot like praying. I write because I feel I have to, I want to. I pray for the same reasons: I have to, I want to. But this doesn't mean I feel like writing (or praying) every day. Some days, I do. (Praise God!) But some days I don't.

Some days I have to make myself write. This means I have to politely remind myself to go and sit down in front of that word processor right now, please. Some days, I can't even afford to be polite. I have to beg or even threaten myself to go write—or else!

Something similar happens with my prayer. Some days I have to convince myself politely to pray. Other days I resort to begging or threatening.

Why bother then? Why bother to write or pray on days I don't feel like doing either?

Why bother? Because I've learned from personal experience: incredible things can happen precisely on those days I didn't feel like writing or praying. I've learned that miraculous things can occur—do occur—when I push myself beyond my immediate inclination. When I make myself write, who knows? A poem or paragraph may come gushing out, one I never knew I had inside of me. And what can happen at prayer? Who knows? I may just run smack into the living, breathing, charming, demanding, immensely attractive, one-of-a-kind Almighty God!

God, for all those times I feel like praying, I say, "Thank you." And for all those times I don't feel like praying, I say, "Please help me to push myself beyond my immediate inclination to risk meeting you."

∞ ∞ ∞

22) Quotes on faith

Faith is a blush in the presence of God. (Abraham Heschel)
Faith is a response to love more than an acceptance of dogma. (Kathleen Norris)
Some things have to be believed to be seen. (Ralph Hodgson)
It is not the dying for faith that's so hard; it's the living up to it that is difficult. (William Thackeray)

God, help me to live up to my faith today by responding to love.

∞ ∞ ∞

23) Letting someone else run the show

When I told her I was looking forward to retreat, she said, "I imagine you'd be looking forward to anything you didn't have to run." She hit the nail right on the head. I am tired of running things and organizing things, whether it be a prayer service, a class, a talk, or a retreat. I just want to sit back, relax, and let someone else run the show.

When I get to heaven, I hope I don't hear St. Peter say, "Welcome, Melannie! You're just in time. Could you please lead a small group discussion tonight on the attributes of God? And I was wondering if you'd like to conduct a retreat next week for new arrivals. And we're making plans for you to teach a seminar to the angels, and...."

If St. Peter does say these things to me, I'll ask, "Hey, Pete! Is this heaven—or is it that other place?"

God, I believe that ultimately you're running the show.

24) A sense of humor

Of all the gifts God could give us, the most valuable might be a sense of humor. In fact, given the option, most of us would probably choose a sense of humor over many of the other gifts God could bestow: intelligence, beauty, leadership skills, patience, athletic prowess, artistic talent, even good health.

Why? Because without a sense of humor, we might be tempted to take ourselves and those other gifts too seriously. And with a sense of humor, we can get along fairly well without those other gifts. So even if we are no Mensa member, we can at least laugh at our mistakes. So we're no beauty; we can chuckle at our imperfect body. So we're not in perfect health; we're still well enough to smile.

I wonder: is a sense of humor more valuable than even the gift of faith? That's probably a moot question, for can we have genuine faith without also having a sense of humor? Don't the two go hand-in-hand? Faith gives us a broader vision of life. So does a sense of humor. Faith enables us to trust in the essential goodness of life. So does humor. Faith helps us to keep things in perspective. So does humor.

In fact, one measure of the wholeness of our faith may be the healthiness of our sense of humor.

God, nourish my sense of humor today.

25) Introduction to grief

Grandma Svoboda used to come and stay with us for a week or so every summer. When she did, my sister and I would take turns sleeping with her in our big double bed. One night, when it was my turn, I was lying beside her, not quite asleep yet, when all of a sudden, I heard something. It was Grandma, and she was crying, softly, but audibly. I was amazed, confused and a little frightened. Up to this point in my life, I thought only kids cried. It never dawned on me that adults cried, too.

The next morning I reported the incident to my father. "Grandma was crying last night in bed," I said in hushed tones.

His response was quick, sure, and gentle. "Sometimes Grandma still misses Grandpa, especially at night," he said.

I couldn't believe what my father had said, because Grandpa had been dead for over ten years. In fact, he died (at age fifty-three) before I was even born. That someone could still miss another person after ten years—and miss him enough to cry—was utterly beyond my comprehension.

Years later I would experience the loss of irreplaceable loved ones, including Grandma Svoboda herself. Only then would I begin to understand why Grandma, as she lay beside me in bed that night, was softly crying.

God, help me to be more understanding of my own grieving and to reach out to someone else who is grieving too.

26) The Bible is not escapist literature

The Bible is not escapist literature. If it were, it would say things like this:

Roses are red, martinis are dry
Sugar is sweet, and so are you and I!

In contrast, the Bible says something like this:

Roses are red, carnations are pink.
We humans can be good, but sometimes we stink!

The truth is, the book we call the Holy Bible has a heck of a lot of sin in it. Why? Because the world has a heck of a lot of sin in it! And the Bible never wants us to forget that fact. For if the Bible is trying to teach us anything, it is this: how to live a good life in the real world, a world brimming over with a lot of goodness, yes, but a world also choking in sin.

We read the Bible, therefore, not solely to be consoled: "I'm okay, you're okay. Aren't we wonderful?" We read the Bible also to be challenged: "I'm not okay. You're not okay. What are we doing about that?"

God, help me to be open to both the challenges and the consolations of the Bible.

27) Honesty and caring

Sometimes we confuse honesty with caring. "I'm just being honest with you," we say after lambasting someone. Or, "It's the truth," we say to justify our insensitive remarks.

Honesty and caring are not the same. You can have honesty without caring, but you can't have caring without honesty. Why is this so? Because caring is honesty plus, and the plus is always this: "I love you." Honesty without the reassurance of this love is not caring at all, and it can do more harm than good. In fact, honesty without love can be a form of violence.

God, help me to be loving in my honesty today.

❧ ❧ ❧

28) Door prizes

Whenever I give talks or retreats, I always give out door prizes. How did this custom begin? It's simple. Years ago, I was asked to give a talk at the National Catholic Educators Association convention in Chicago. I was a nobody in the field of education on a roster of superstars. "No one's going to come to my talk!" I pouted. That's when I got the idea: "I know! I'll give out door prizes! Then people will come!" So, at the end of the blurb describing my talk, I wrote, "Free door prizes will be awarded." Imagine my surprise when I walked into the room that day and found it packed with over two hundred people! To this day I maintain that what attracted such a horde was not me or my topic. It was the door prizes!

That's why I began giving out door prizes. But it's not the reason I continue to do so. As I explain to my groups, all around us are ordinary and natural signs of extraordinary spiritual realities. To me, door prizes are one such sign, a symbol of God's gratuitous love. Think about it. We don't have to do anything to win a door prize. We don't have to answer a tough question, sing a song, or do a dance. We don't even have to pay for a chance. All we have to do is to scribble our name on a ticket, and that's it.

Door prizes are a lot like God's love. We do not earn God's love. We do not have to do something difficult to get it. God's love is gratuitous, that is, freely given. In a way, then, we can say we have all won the door prize of the gift of life. It's as if God said to each one of us, "Here's a life! Do something beautiful with it!"

God, help me to do something beautiful today with my door prize of life.

❧ ❧ ❧

29) Learning obedience through beauty

Anne Morrow Lindbergh wrote that she used to think one came to true learning, understanding, and vision through suffering. But now she believes one learns these things "through suffering and beauty. One alone won't do it."

In the letter to the Hebrews we find these words describing Jesus: "Although he was a Son, he learned obedience through what he suffered" (Heb 5:8). The word "obedience" here means basically being at one with God's will. Scripture is saying, therefore, that Jesus came to know and embrace the will of God through suffering. But if what Lindbergh says is true, did Jesus also learn obedience through beauty?

I think the answer is "yes." We cannot read the gospels without concluding that Jesus loved beauty, all kinds of beauty. He appreciated, for example, the beauty in nature. Like many of us, Jesus sometimes stood and gazed off into the distance, sensing intuitively a vista's power to calm or inspire, whether the vista included bobbing lilies, golden wheat fields, a bustling city, or a glistening sea. From his words, we know Jesus was attuned to the beauty of changing weather and seasons, both subtle and dramatic. As a carpenter, he appreciated beautiful wood. As a human being, he delighted in a beautiful meal. After all, he wasn't labeled a glutton for nothing!

Jesus appreciated the beauty of animals, too. He began his life with sheep and cattle in a stable. And when he entered Jerusalem for the last time, he was riding on a donkey. Jesus must have loved animals to incorporate so many of them into his teachings: sheep, goats, cattle, camels, wolves, swine, snakes, doves, sea monsters, fish, chickens, and even dogs and puppies.

But it was primarily in his dealings with people that Jesus came to know and appreciate beauty: the beauty of parents devoted to their children, the beauty of a Roman soldier concerned for his slave, the beauty of a leper grateful for a cure, the beauty of a poor widow generous beyond measure, the beauty of friends to encourage and support, the beauty of disciples to leave all and follow.

Yes, Jesus learned obedience through suffering; but he also came to know and embrace God's will through beauty.

Jesus, help me to learn obedience through both suffering and beauty.

❧ ❧ ❧

30) Hobo signs

Years ago, hobos had the custom of leaving messages for one another along the road. Devising their own system of symbols, they scrawled these messages with chalk on fenceposts, barns, train stations, and other places. A simple cross, for example, meant "angel food" and indicated a place that offered temporary shelter and a free meal—provided you sat through a sermon first. A triangle with upraised arms marked a home where the owner had a gun. A sketch that resembled a comb warned of a mean dog with vicious teeth.

We Christians are something like those hobos, for we, too, are on a journey far from a place we can call home. Wending our way on our earthly pilgrimage, we know full well that both dangers and opportunities lie all around us. But we need help in discerning which is which. We need signs to steer us clear of mean dogs and to direct us to temporary housing and free meals. Fortunately, other "hobos" have gone before us and helped mark the way, most notably the saints. Their lives as well as their writings are like messages scrawled in chalk to help guide us on our journey home.

God, make me more attentive to the messages your saints have scrawled for me.

❧ ❧ ❧

31) Two kids on a slide

I glanced out my window yesterday afternoon and saw two small children on the playground below. The little girl was about eight; the boy (her little brother, I concluded) was about three. The girl had just finished going down the slide. Having watched her, the little boy scampered to the steps of the slide and began climbing them, while his sister stood at the end of the slide waiting.

The higher the boy climbed, the slower he went, obviously afraid. Yet, with his sister yelling words of encouragement at him, the boy continued to climb. Arriving at the top, he sat down gingerly. His sister, holding wide her arms to receive him, began coaxing him to slide down. For a few seconds, the boy sat poised there, as if carefully deciding what to do next. Suddenly, he gave himself a big push. In a flash he was down the slide and crashing into his sister below. The impact almost knocked her over, but somehow, she managed to keep herself—and her little brother—from falling over.

How much we rely on the encouragement of others to do the hard things in life, I thought. In this case, if it hadn't been for his sister, that little boy probably would never have gone down that slide. To accomplish that feat, he first had to see his sister do it. Then he needed her encouragement as well as her presence at the end of the slide, waiting with open arms to catch him.

Jesus goes before us. And he waits for us—with open arms—at the end of our slide.

Jesus, you encourage me to do the hard things in life by going before me and waiting for me with open arms.

32) Mary's prayer at Cana

Mary's request at the wedding feast of Cana reminds us that we do not have to resort to convoluted explanations when we ask God for things. We do not necessarily have to go into detail. Sometimes a simple statement of fact will do.

"They have no wine," Mary says (Jn 2:3). Having stated that, she leaves everything else in Jesus' hands.

Sometimes our prayer can be like that: "So-and-so is ill...People are hurting...I'm really worried about him (her)...I'm lonely...." Just state the fact and let Jesus act.

Of course, we must be willing to accept the action Jesus decides to take, even when he appears to take no action at all, or (just as difficult) when he appears to be asking us to take action.

Jesus, let my prayer be simple statements of fact today, and help me to accept whatever action you decide to take.

33) Midsummer's Day dialogues

June 22 is the time of the summer solstice in the northern hemisphere. It is also known as "midsummer's day." According to legend, this is the time of year when the veil that separates the various life forms on earth is the thinnest, making communication between them the easiest.

This is the day when Ms. Dandelion can dialogue with Mr. Worm, when Herr Goose can chat with Old Man Willow, and when human beings can converse effortlessly with the stars. Believing this to be true, I go outside this afternoon to dialogue with some of the other life forms—and the so-called "inanimate" forms as well—asking them to share their wisdom with me.

I enter the cow pasture and chance upon a bevy of bright yellow buttercups bobbing in the breeze. "Speak to me, O buttercups!" I say. "Share some of your wisdom with me, please!"

The buttercups reply, "The cows never eat us. Know why? Because of our beauty!"

I know better, of course. And for a split second I'm tempted to set the buttercups straight. "The cows couldn't care less about your beauty," I want to say. "It's your awful taste that drives the cows away." But not today. Not on midsummer's day. Today it is not my place to educate buttercups. It's my place to be instructed by them, and so I listen on.

Good thing, too, for I hear the buttercups say to me, "So, remember this: it is our beauty that enables us to survive and thrive. Beauty is essential for survival and growth. Our wisdom for you? Always make room for beauty in your life: in your home, your work, your leisure, your relationships, your prayer. No beauty, no life."

I thank the buttercups for their wisdom—and their beauty—and I move on to chat with other life forms.

God, help me to make room for beauty in my world today.

34) Dialogue with a herd of cows

Next I come to a herd of cows standing under some trees at the edge of the pasture. "Good afternoon, Lady Cows," I say. "Would you mind sharing some of your wisdom with me?"

"Keep your fanny to the wind," says the first cow.

"Never wander too far from the herd," says the second.

"If it's hot—like today—seek shade," says a third.

"The flies are terrible," says another as she swishes her tail back and forth and all around. "But tails and ears do help. And don't think it's beneath your dignity to rub up against Brother Tree at times or to lumber into Sister Creek. And, over the years, we cows have learned this little trick to get relief from the flies: we stand head to tail with our fellow cows. When we do this, we can take advantage of our sisters' swatting tails to get rid of those pesky flies that neither our own ears nor our own tail can reach."

"Ruminate, ruminate, ruminate," says another cow as she chews her cud contentedly.

"Thank you for your wisdom, Lady Cows," I say as I start to walk away. "I'll ruminate, ruminate, ruminate on everything you've said to me." And I do.

God, lead me to ruminate on nature's wisdom today.

❧ ❧ ❧

35) Dialogue with Grandpa Willow Tree

I seek out Grandpa Willow standing near the edge of Sister Creek. With his massive trunk and gnarled branches, he is more stump now than towering tree. Yet dozens of lush green branches sprout from his broken limbs and torso.

"Greetings, Grandpa Willow," I say. "Would you please share your wisdom with me today?"

"How long have you got, young'un?" he asks.

"Young'un?!" I protest. "But I'm over fifty!"

"And I'm over one hundred!" he replies proudly.

I bow to him. "I guess I am young, compared to you," I say with respect.

Seeing my deference, Grandpa Willow begins to share his wisdom with me. He speaks slowly, in short, declarative sentences, the language of the truly wise.

"Every knot's a story," he says. "Every gnarl's a blessing. One day at a time. Perseverance comes mostly from within. Stay close to your water supply. Be generous with your branches and your shade. Bend, bend, bend. Broken branches are a matter of course: don't fret their loss. New ones are sure to sprout in their place. Look at all of mine!" and he shakes his new growth in the breeze.

I thank Grandpa Willow for his bountiful wisdom. With reluctance, I take my leave of him.

God, help me to absorb some of Grandpa Willow's wisdom.

36) The miracle of flight and life

The more we fly, the more likely we are to take flying for granted. I have heard seasoned flyers saying things like this at the check-in counter:

"You mean the flight is thirty minutes late?"

"But I wanted an aisle seat, not a window!"

"What do you mean I have to check this bag?"

"I hate full flights!"

"You mean all we get on this flight is a lousy sandwich?"

They can let the minor inconveniences of flying blind them to the incredible miracle of flight.

The same can happen with living. The longer we live, the more likely we are to take living for granted. We can let minor inconveniences blind us to the incredible miracle of life itself. I imagine some of us saying things like this at the check-in counter of life:

"You mean I've got to be born into *that* family?"

"But I wanted to be tall, not short!"

"What do you mean I have to work for a living?"

"But I hate headaches! And I don't want arthritis!"

"You mean I have to eat green beans?"

God, may the minor inconveniences of living never blind me to the incredible miracle of life.

37) A Hasidic story

A father complained to the Baalshem that his son had forgotten God. "What, Rabbi, should I do?" he asked. The Baalshem answered, "Love him more than ever."

It was columnist Erma Bombeck who wrote something similar: it is when our children deserve our love the least that they need it the most.

God, help me to see who needs my love the most today.

38) Only God?

At the end of the book of Micah we find this beautiful prayer:

Shepherd your people with your staff, the flock that belongs to you....Who is a God like you, pardoning iniquity and passing over the transgression of the remnant of your possession?...(You) delight in showing clemency. (You) will again have compassion upon us....You will cast all our sins into the depths of the sea. (Mi 7:14, 18–19)

What makes this prayer so noteworthy are the circumstances under which is was composed. It was written right after the chosen people returned from their exile in Babylon. This time was, indeed, one of the lowest points in their entire history. They had been totally humiliated by their enemy, their population had been decimated, and their land was snatched away. In addition, they were surrounded on all sides by hostile forces. In short, they were a people without hope, without a future. Yet they could pray a prayer like this one, filled with absolute trust in God's goodness and mercy.

In one way, this is remarkable. But in another way, it is not surprising at all. For, at this nadir in their history, the people had nothing left to trust in. Everything had been taken away from them: their reputation, numbers, land, power, and even a hopeful future. They had nothing, only God.

Only God? Sometimes our prayer is at its best when our lives are at their worst.

God, I will trust you today—only you.

☙ ☙ ☙

39) Thank God for words

She asks, "What's he like?"

And my words come tumbling out. No, some come tumbling. Others come hopping and skipping and soaring forth in their eagerness to describe you, my new friend. And not until this moment do I realize just how much you already mean to me. It's as if in telling her about you, I am meeting you—really meeting you—for the first time. It's as if my saying of the words is enabling me to love you even more.

Thank God for good questions! Thank God for good attempts at answers! Most of all, thank God for words! For, as inadequate as they may be at times, words are still one of the best ways we humans have for knowing what we think, for realizing what we believe, and for appreciating what and whom we love.

God, help me to use words more gratefully today.

40) Quotes on adversity

Adversity causes some people to break, others to break records. (William Arthur Ward)

The art of living is more like wrestling than dancing. (Marcus Aurelius)

Adversity is the first path to truth. (Lord Byron)

A diamond is a chunk of coal that made good under pressure. (Anonymous)

God did not say, "You shall not be tempest-tossed, you shall not be work-weary, you shall not be discomforted." But God said, "You shall not be overcome." (Julian of Norwich)

God, help me to face adversity today by trusting in your strength rather than in my own.

41) Jesus did not carry a pocket calendar

Jesus did not carry a pocket calendar. He did not wear a watch. He didn't say, "Sorry, Lazarus. I can't make it Friday evening. Board meeting." Or, "Sorry, Martha, Mary. Saturday's out. I have to write those Beatitudes, you know."

When the women brought their children to Jesus for a blessing, he didn't look at his watch and say, "Well, okay, let the little children come to me, but only for five minutes." And when Nicodemus came to him at night, Jesus didn't say, "Look, Nick, it's after ten already. How 'bout coming back tomorrow morning during office hours? I can squeeze you in from 11:00 to 11:15."

How free are *we* in relating to others? Have efficiency and productivity become our top priorities? Do we run our families and personal relationships like small businesses? Are our parishes and church beginning to look more and more like big corporations?

Dates are important. Appointments are necessary. Order has its place. But do we allow them to rule our entire lives?

Jesus, help me to be freer in relating to others today.

✎ ✎ ✎

42) Accepting talents and limitations

We must learn to accept both our talents and our limitations. Ironically, it is sometimes easier for us to accept the latter than the former. Why? In accepting our limitations we are left off the hook, so to speak. The admission, "I can't draw a straight line with a ruler," for example, releases us from any obligation to draw. "I can't dance," allows us to sit complacently at the edge of the dance floor.

Talents, on the other hand, call us to action, to service. You can write? Then why not write a book? You can cook? Then shouldn't you be inviting friends in for dinner? You can sing? Then join the church choir, for heaven's sake!

The truth is that talents are not the opposite of limitations. Most so-called talented individuals work very hard at what they do. Professional ice skaters, for example, take to the ice every morning, show or no show. Professional athletes spend many hours off the field working out in the weight room. Writers devote hours to research and rewriting. In other words, so-called talented people are always pushing themselves—and their art—beyond the very real limitations of time, energy, and innate skill.

A good question to ask ourselves is this: are we too quick to accept as a limitation what may, in fact, be the outer edge of a latent talent?

God, help me to use one of my talents today to serve others.

✍ ✍ ✍

43) Gravity is our friend

"Gravity is our friend." That's what Mrs. House taught us in third grade. Gravity is what keeps the people in Australia from falling off the globe, she pointed out. I noted that even those of us living in Ohio, USA, needed gravity, too, or we'd probably slide all the way down to Georgia. Yes, gravity was our friend. It kept us stuck to the earth where we belonged. And that was good. At least that's what I thought until the day I wanted to fly.

That's the day Jimmy, Kenny, Pauly, and I got a ladder from somewhere and used it to climb up onto the flat chicken coop roof. It was pretty high up there and we were enjoying the view when, before I knew it, those boys were daring me to jump off the roof and fly. Remembering what Mrs. House said about gravity, I hesitated. That's when they double-dared me. So I thought, who knows? If gravity was indeed our friend, as Mrs. House said it was, they maybe it would loosen its hold on me—just this once—so that I could fly up into the clouds and show those boys once and for all.

While I was thinking about this, those boys triple-dared me, so I had no choice. I had to jump. I had to try to fly. Gritting my teeth, I took a running start and *SWOOSH!* I was in the air before I had the chance to change my mind. For one split second I thought my friend gravity had, indeed, released its hold on me and I was really going to impress those boys with my soaring. But no. Gravity yanked me back to earth and I hit the ground with a THUD! crumbling into a little heap in the dirt. So much for gravity's friendship.

Even before I moved, I knew I had hurt one leg a little, but not wanting the boys to know, I jumped up quickly and yelled a big lie to the three of them gaping down at me: "That was FUUUN!" And I quickly hobbled back to the ladder, knowing now I had to jump a second time to prove I really meant it when I said it was fun. I was halfway up the ladder when Jimmy's mother came out onto the back porch and yelled, "YOU KIDS GET OFF THE ROOF THIS INSTANT!" Immediately I hobbled back down the ladder with a big secret sigh of relief.

To this day I still have my doubts about what Mrs. House taught us, that gravity is our friend. That's because I still believe, in the end, we are all meant to soar.

God, reveal to me those things in my life that keep me tied down and prevent me from soaring freely.

☙ ☙ ☙

44) Sensitivity: the art of the small

Sometimes we think sensitivity is more cross than gift. "If I weren't so sensitive," we reason, "I wouldn't feel this pain." Even though sensitivity can cause pain, it is still a gift, and one that is absolutely essential for Christian living. After all, most of the good that is done in the world is the direct result of somebody's sensitivity.

Carlos Valles, SJ, calls sensitivity "the art of the small." He's right. Ordinarily, sensitivity is not expressed in sweeping movements, but in little gestures: the attentive look, the kind interpretation, the simple word, the small token, the gentle touch.

Jesus was sensitive. For example, he worked his first miracle at a wedding reception, just to save a young couple from embarrassment (Jn 2:1–11). While being mobbed by a crowd, Jesus was sensitive to the tassel-touching of the woman with the hemorrhage (Lk 8:43–48). And of all those individuals standing outside the temple treasury that one day watching the people depositing their offerings, only Jesus seemed to notice the poor widow with her two small coins and (what's even more remarkable) was able to instantly assess their real worth (Mk 12:41–44).

We need never apologize or feel bad for being sensitive. Jesus himself was master of this art of the small.

Jesus, help me to be sensitive today, to master this art of the small, like you.

❧ ❧ ❧

45) The pristine ministry of conversation

The gospels frequently show Jesus conversing with people. When the two disciples of John the Baptist meet Jesus for the first time, they ask him, "Rabbi, where are you staying?" Jesus replies, "Come and you will see" (Jn 1:38–39). The two disciples go with Jesus and spend the entire day with him. What did the three men do together that day if not simply talk with one another?

Something similar happens to the man in the land of the Gerasenes who was possessed by a legion of demons. After he was cured by Jesus, the man sits down and converses with Jesus (Lk 8:35). Other individuals in the gospels were also changed for the better simply by having a good conversation with Jesus: Nicodemus, Zacchaeus, the woman at the well, Mary and Martha, the disciples on the road to Emmaus, to name a few.

Today we tend to think of evangelization in terms of teaching and preaching, that is, in terms of talking to people or, worse yet, talking *at* people. But Jesus shows us another way: the art of conversation. Jesus did teach and preach, of course, but he also spent considerable time simply talking with people. He asked them questions, listened to their stories, answered their questions, and shared his own thoughts and feelings with them.

If we wish to become more effective evangelizers, then maybe we have to work at reclaiming the pristine ministry of conversation.

Jesus, teach me the pristine ministry of conversation.

☙ ☙ ☙

46) The chaplain at the children's hospital

Sister Rose is a chaplain at a children's hospital. Everyday she ministers to sick and dying children and their families. In the morning she holds the hand of Troy, a four-year-old swathed in bandages in the burn unit. "He's not going to make it," a nurse whispers to her as she leaves the unit.

At noon she feeds a bottle to Justin, an eight-month-old with AIDS, staying long enough to rock him to sleep. This afternoon she cradles a sobbing mother, Carmelita, whose ten-year-old daughter has just been diagnosed with leukemia. And right before leaving, she helps two stunned parents with the funeral arrangements for their daughter, age five, who ran out in front of a car.

And when Sister Rose comes home tonight, one of us greets her with, "You're late." Another one complains, "The coffee maker's not working again." And the third one asks, "Isn't this rain depressing?"

God, help me to keep things in perspective today.

∞ ∞ ∞

47) Crowns, hearts, and feet in the Bible

Several years ago, when my dentist put in my first crown, I suddenly noticed (for the first time) how many times the word "crown" appears in the psalms I was praying every day:

You...crowned them with glory and honor (Ps 8:5).
You set a crown of fine gold on his head (Ps 21:3).
You crown the year with your bounty (Ps 65:11).

Similarly, after I had an echocardiogram, I suddenly became aware of how many times the word "heart" also shows up:

You have put gladness in my heart (Ps 4:7).
My heart shall not fear (Ps 27:3).
Create in me a clean heart, O God (Ps 51:10).
Search me, O God, and know my heart (Ps 139:23).

I suppose if I have foot surgery someday, I will notice the following lines in the psalms:

You have set my feet in a broad place (Ps 31:8).
For you have delivered my soul from death, and my feet from falling (Ps 56:13).
Your word is a lamp to my feet (Ps 119:105).

The point is, we are not meant to read the psalms—or any other part of the Bible, for that matter—in a vacuum. We are meant to bring to our reading whatever may be happening in our personal lives. Reading scripture becomes fruitful only when we bring to it the events and concerns of our immediate experience.

God, help me to bring the events and concerns of my immediate experience to the scripture I read today.

48) The roar of the ordinary

One of the greatest gifts God has given me is my love for the ordinary. Vanilla ice cream, daisies, and even a glass of water often bring me just as much joy and pleasure as baked Alaska, long-stemmed red roses, and fine French wine.

I feel sorry for people who overlook the ordinary, who don't appreciate the everyday, who need the exotic to experience pleasure. In her novel *Middlemarch*, George Eliot writes, "If we had a keen vision and a feeling of all ordinary human life, it would be like hearing the grass grow and the squirrel's heart beat, and we should die of that roar which lies on the other side of silence."

Happy are they who have a keen feel for everyday human life, whose ears are attuned to the roar of the ordinary. Happy are they who get a kick out of the commonplace, for they shall bump into joy and pleasure wherever they go!

God, increase in me a love for the ordinary.

Last eve I saw a beauty contest brief
Between a rainbow and an autumn leaf.

—*Anonymous*

FALL

49) Jesus saves

One of the first controversies in the early church is recorded in the Acts of the Apostles. It seems that certain individuals were teaching, "Unless you are circumcised according to the custom of Moses, you cannot be saved" (Acts 15:1). The apostles and elders finally had to meet in Jerusalem to settle the dispute.

Peter and others strongly opposed the view that converts to Christianity had to submit to circumcision. "We believe that we will be saved through the grace of the Lord Jesus," Peter said emphatically. In other words, Jesus saves—and not ritual or law. In the end, Peter's thinking prevailed.

At first glance this ancient controversy may seem pretty tame to us, perhaps even quaint. We might be tempted to say, "That's a far cry from the controversies in the current church!" But is it really? Don't we continue to struggle with the same underlying question: who (or what) saves us? Aren't we still tempted to substitute other things for Jesus?

What things? Here are a few: Virtue saves. Education saves. Obedience saves. A certain method of prayer saves. A specific way of celebrating liturgy saves. This theologian saves. Gender saves. Liberalism saves. Conservatism saves. Or even: I save myself!

Maybe we need to hear Peter's words again today: "We will be saved through the grace of the Lord Jesus."

Jesus, strengthen my conviction that you alone are my savior.

❧ ❧ ❧

50) God as Father, Grandma, and Coach

Jesus said, "Pray then in this way: Our Father in heaven…" (Mt 6:9). Jesus encouraged his disciples to think of God in terms of Father. He himself quite readily addressed God as Abba, that is, "Daddy."

Those of us blessed with a good father have no difficulty in thinking of God in terms of father. Similarly, those of us blessed with a fine mother have little problem thinking of God as mother. But what about those individuals who never had a good father or mother? What about those whose parents were negligent or even abusive? How do these people address God?

The answer to that question can be found by asking another question: who mirrors God's love for us? For the bottom line is this: whoever has loved us, there is God.

When we pray, many of us, therefore, can easily address God as father or mother. But others will find it more meaningful to address God as Grandma or Grandpa. Others may prefer to call God Aunt or Uncle, Brother or Sister, Teacher, Coach, or even Friend.

But no human being, no matter how good they are to us, mirrors God's love perfectly. Even the best parent falls short, the most devoted friend disappoints us. That's why we might not want to restrict our image of God to only one person: Mother, Father, Grandma. In fact, our prayer might prove richer if we vary, on a regular basis, the way we address God. One day, we might address God as Father. Another day, as Grandma. And still another day we might call God Coach.

God, help me to reflect on those individuals who mirror your love for me that I may address you in those terms.

❧ ❧ ❧

51) Geese are not dumb

A man was outside in his yard raking leaves with his little boy. Suddenly a flock of wild geese flew overhead, on their way south for the winter. "Look at the geese!" the man called to his son. "See how they're flying in a vee?" he pointed out.

The boy stared up in amazement, "Wow!" he exclaimed. Then he asked his father, "Do they know any other letters?"

We smile at the little boy's remark. Of course geese don't know any other letters. When it comes to knowing the alphabet, geese are dumb! But, it's good to remind ourselves that when it comes to other things, geese are far from dumb. After all, they do manage to migrate each year across thousands of miles of terrain—much of it inhospitable. And they make the long journey without map, compass, or suitcase and without benefit of restaurants and motels along the way. And somewhere in their past, geese also figured out the laws of physics—at least enough to fly in a V-formation to utilize those laws to their advantage.

St. Francis of Assisi said that all aspects of creation—including the animals—are holy. He even went so far as to dub everything brother and sister. Animals have much to teach us if we take the time to get to know them as our brothers and sisters.

God, help me to know my animal brothers and sisters better—either directly through observation or indirectly through reading or watching TV—that I may learn from them.

❧ ❧ ❧

52) Wait and see

Someone has said that when it comes to deciding whether or not to do something, we have three choices: 1) Do it. 2) Delegate it. 3) Ditch it. But isn't there a fourth? Delay it. In other words, wait and see. Some might say that delaying things or waiting for things to happen is procrastination, and procrastination is unhealthy. Maybe so. Maybe not.

All delaying is not procrastination. All waiting is not unhealthy. Even Jesus warned against taking rash action. In his parable of the wheat and the weeds, for example, he cautions against madly tearing into a field of wheat to yank out all the weeds (Mt 13:24–30). "Wait until the harvest," he urges. "Lest you pull up the precious wheat with the weeds."

As Christians, there are times we will be called to act; that is, to do it, delegate it, or ditch it. But such actions must always be balanced with our willingness to wait and see.

God, teach me to wait and see.

❧ ❧ ❧

53) Proverbs

If someone throws stones at you, throw back bread. (Yiddish proverb)

Be not afraid of growing slowly; be afraid only of standing still. (Chinese proverb)

Custom without reason is but ancient error. (English proverb)

The reverse side also has a reverse side. (Japanese proverb)

A mountain shames a molehill until they both are humbled by the stars. (Anonymous)

A good laugh and a long sleep are two best cures. (Irish proverb)

God, speak to me today through the wisdom of these proverbs.

❧ ❧ ❧

54) George Dawson, 98

George Dawson of Dallas, the grandson of a slave, attended school for the first time at age 98. What prompted him to start school so late in life? "I was lost in a sea of words," he explained. "And I'd like to be able to read my Bible."

George Dawson reminds us that we are never too old to start something new. Granted, some things are more difficult to do with age, but such things are probably fewer than we imagine. A nun friend of mine, for example, started to swim at age 70. Another friend started her writing career at age 76. Even in the Bible we have the example of Abraham who, at 70, was called by God to start a whole new life in a brand new land.

The philosopher Martin Buber said it well: "To be old is a glorious thing when one has not unlearned what it means 'to begin.'"

God, help me to begin something new today.

❧ ❧ ❧

55) The anatomy lesson

She and I sat together after supper looking at her anatomy book. "Just look at all the muscles we have!" she said pointing to the drawings. "Did you know we use over twenty muscles in the face just to smile?"

I told her I didn't. For several minutes, then, we studied the facial muscles, and then we went on to admire the intricacies of a single tooth.

Flipping the pages forward again, she said with excitement, "Wait till I show you the small intestine. It's really neat!" And she spread the drawings of the small intestine before me and went on to explain some of its functions. In all, we sat there for over an hour poring over that book.

That night, I prayed for this young biology student. I prayed that when she becomes a teacher, she will pass on to her students not only her knowledge of biological facts, but, more importantly, her sense of wonder at all of them.

God, thank you for the wonder of the human body.

56) God's good company

Why do we pray? Really?

For many reasons, I'm sure. But the basic reason, I think, is this: we pray to put ourselves in the presence of someone who is absolutely favorably disposed toward us. Quite simply, we pray in order to be with someone who loves us, adores us, delights in us, thinks the world of us. Namely, God.

Think of it in human terms. We go to a big party and step into a room filled with scores of people we know. To whom do we instinctively gravitate? To Joe Blow over there who we know can't stand us? To Hector What's-his-name over there who barely knows us? Or to Sally Clapsaddle over there who's known us for years and really, really likes us? The answer is obvious: we head for Sally.

When we go to prayer, we are seeking out Someone who's known us forever and likes us more than any other person does or could. Why would we not eagerly seek out such good company? Why do we not run to prayer?

God, thank you for your good company!

❧ ❧ ❧

57) Solving problems with a harp

One of my favorite lines in the psalms is this: "I will solve my riddle to the music of the harp" (Ps 49:4). Another translation says, "I will solve my problem with the music of a harp." The riddle or problem that the psalmist is talking about is the problem of evil in the world. More specifically, the psalmist is questioning why the wicked seem to triumph while the good are made to suffer.

That verse from the psalm is a good one to call to mind whenever we are beset with our own particular problems or riddles in life. "I will solve my problem with a harp." Do we ever let music help us to solve our difficulties?

Probably most of us instinctively reach for reason to solve our problems. That is, we think about our problems, analyze them, and sometimes even agonize over them. In addition, we often seek the advice of others. We go from person to person in an attempt to find someone who will solve our problem for us. Or we may also seek solutions by reading a book or attending a class or lecture. Though all of these ways may be helpful, we might also want to consider the way of the psalmist, namely, music.

Listening to music can ease our minds and soothe our hearts—which just might help us to solve our problems more easily, or at least enable us to face them with greater patience and trust. Listening to or singing religious songs might be particularly helpful in directing us to some action or in simply reminding us of God's everlasting love for us.

"I will solve my problem with a harp"—or piano, or guitar, or flute, or complete orchestra, or even by singing slowly and softly, "Amazing grace, how sweet the sound...."

God, help me to make time for music today.

❦ ❦ ❦

58) Writing a book

Writing a book is a lot like having a baby. (Being a nun, I've never had a baby myself, but I have "had" several books.) First, there's that moment of conception. Conception can happen at any time—even when you don't expect it or haven't planned it. I conceived the idea for one of my books while blow-drying my hair in the bathroom!

Next comes the pregnancy. Working on a book has its own version of morning sickness: words won't come, paragraphs fizzle, ideas dry up, you get discouraged and depressed, and all the while you're beginning to realize that a completely new and independent life is growing inside of you, growing because of you and, simultaneously, growing despite you. Then there's all the care you take to foster this new life—the people you seek out for encouragement and advice, the books you do and don't read. Other individuals are also involved in the development of your unborn child. Friends, editors, and proofreaders act as doctors and midwives. Seeing the proofs of your book is a lot like viewing a sonogram, for that's when you first catch a glimpse of your baby's shape and form.

There are labor pains throughout the writing process: the endless rewriting, the continuous striving for accuracy, the tedious proofreading, the meticulous attention to detail. Finally, the moment of birth arrives. I treasure that moment when the small box arrives from my publisher containing several advance copies of my book. I ritualize the opening of the box with prayer, thanking God for everyone who helped me to bring forth this child, and asking God to bless everyone who will eventually read this book. Finally, I open the box, pick up a copy of my book, examine it lovingly, and press it to my heart with gratitude and joy.

Writing a book is like giving birth. So are a lot of other worthwhile things.

God, make me more attentive to whatever I am giving birth to in my life.

❧ ❧ ❧

59) Things I've learned as a teacher

After twenty-five years of teaching, I've learned many things. Here are a few of them:

1) I've learned that I don't teach English, history, or religion; I teach people.

2) I've learned that if I expect good things from my students, I am more likely to get good things.

3) I've learned it is more important for me to know my students than it is for me to know my subject matter.

4) I've learned that the best sign that my students are learning something in my class is if we laugh together on a regular basis.

5) I've learned that discipline is a by-product of these two factors: conscientious preparation for class and genuine love and respect for my students.

6) I've learned that no teacher ever had the ideal students, schedule, materials, or environment—not even Jesus!

God, lead me to articulate what I have learned from my work or ministry.

❧ ❧ ❧

60) Jesus never said, "I told you so!"

...and it's not because he didn't have ample opportunity, either. When he arrives at the home of Jairus, for example, he is told that Jairus' daughter is already dead. Jesus says to the mourners gathered there, "The child is not dead but sleeping" (Mk 5:39). Hearing this, the crowd laughs Jesus to scorn. We all know what happens next. Jesus raises the little girl from the dead and, instead of saying to the crowd, "See, I told you so!" he says to her parents, "Give her something to eat."

Another time Jesus could have said, "I told you so!" was after the resurrection when the apostles were cowering in the upper room. Jesus suddenly appears in their midst and says to them, "Peace be with you." Then he commissions them: "As the Father has sent me, so I send you" (Jn 20:19–21). Later, on the shore of the sea of Galilee, Jesus singles out Peter, the one person to whom he had every right to say, "See? I told you you would betray me! I told you I would rise!" But instead, Jesus asks, "Simon, son of John, do you love me?" And when Peter humbly professes his love, Jesus says, "Feed my sheep" (Jn 21:16–17).

The lesson is clear. Instead of saying, "I told you so" to individuals who were proven wrong, Jesus gave them a second chance. By entrusting them with a new responsibility, he offered them the opportunity to reclaim their self-esteem and to prove anew their love.

God, help me to give someone a second chance today.

❧ ❧ ❧

61) We know who holds the future

There is probably nothing we humans fear more than the future. Just look at how many office buildings in this country belong to insurance companies. The viability of so many companies is directly attributable to our basic fear of tomorrow, a fear that causes us to spend billions of dollars each year trying to insure ourselves against minor setbacks or major catastrophes.

This fear of the future also explains our fascination with those individuals who claim to be able to predict the future. If anyone really could predict the future with any degree of accuracy, he or she would be worshiped as a god.

How do we face this unknown and often foreboding future with any degree of equilibrium? By trusting in God. For God is not only the God of the past and the present, God is also the God of the future. The old maxim says it well: "We don't know what the future holds, but we know who holds the future." Or another one: "Don't be afraid of tomorrow. God is already there."

God, may I entrust all my fears of the future to you, the One who holds the future.

❧ ❧ ❧

62) Quotes on friendship

Two are better than one...For if they fall, one will lift up the other; but woe to one who is alone and falls and does not have another to help. (Eccl 4:9–10)

One does not make friends. One recognizes them. (Garth Henrichs)

If you want an accounting of your worth, count your friends. (Merry Browne)

No matter what accomplishments you achieve, someone helps you. (Althea Gibson)

True happiness consists not in the multitude of friends, but in their worth and choice. (Ben Jonson)

A true friend never gets in your way unless you happen to be going down. (Arnold Glasow)

Thank you, God, for my friends. Help me to reach out to one of them today.

❧ ❧ ❧

63) Heaven is coming home

On my way home from the meeting, I decide to stop in to see Mom and Dad. It's a cold, dark November evening. Suppertime. As I pull into the driveway, I see lights on in the kitchen. Through the window I spot Dad in his red plaid flannel shirt, sitting at the table with his newspaper. Mom, aproned, is standing by the stove stirring something—homemade leek soup, perhaps. Dad, catching sight of me through the window, smiles and stands up stiffly and slightly stooped. As I step up onto the back porch, Dad opens the door wide and announces cheerfully, "Well, look who's here!" And I step into the warmth of that kitchen and into the warmth of their embraces.

That's what it's going to be like when I die and enter heaven. It will be like stepping out of the cold and darkness, into the warmth and brightness of a homey kitchen, with Mom and Dad there waiting for me. And they will both smile when they see me and open wide their arms. And Dad will announce cheerfully, "Well, look who's here!"

God, may I keep before myself a clear, strong image of entering heaven.

❧ ❧ ❧

64) What's wrong with God

Sometimes I say to God: "You know what's wrong with you?"

And God asks, "What?"

And I begin to enumerate. "You love too indiscriminately. You trust people way too much. You're far too forgiving. And you're entirely too patient!"

Having said that, I invite God to tell me what's wrong with me. But all I hear God say is, "You know, Honey, I really get a kick out of you!"

Which only proves my point.

God, thank you for loving me so much.

❧ ❧ ❧

65) The popular cow

A certain farmer had a cow that was very much loved by his family and neighbors. He also had a pig that wasn't as popular. One day the pig said to the cow, "How come everybody likes you so much? People say you're generous because you give milk, butter, and cream every day. Heck! I give more than that. I give bacon and ham. And you can even pickle my feet! Yet, I'm not as popular as you are. Why?"

Said the cow, "Maybe it's because I give while I'm still alive."

What we give after we're dead means little. What really counts is what we give of ourselves, how much we love, while we're still alive.

God, help me to give of myself to others today—while I'm still alive.

❦ ❦ ❦

66) St. Francis of Assisi had a sweet tooth

Most people don't know that St. Francis of Assisi had a sweet tooth. In fact, he had a special fondness for marchpane, a popular candy of his day made from crushed almonds, cream, sugar, and egg whites. Tradition says that, as he lay dying, Francis asked his friends to notify his friend Lady Jacqueline of Settesoli of his condition. Then he added, "Tell her to send me some marchpane—the kind she has made for me many times in the past." According to the story, Lady Jacqueline was already on her way with a basketful of them for her friend Francis.

There's something consoling in this picture of the austere Francis of Assisi munching on candy on his deathbed. We do the saints a disservice when we emphasize only their austerity and not their humanity, when we stress only how much they are unlike us rather than how much we have in common with them.

God, teach me to know the saints better, that I may appreciate what I have in common with them.

❦ ❦ ❦

67) The promise of ultimate victory

Jesus promises us ultimate victory—the victory of life over death, good over evil, joy over sorrow. Victory, ultimate victory. But what exactly is meant by ultimate victory? It means final victory, conclusive victory, in-the-end victory. Victory not necessarily today, nor even tomorrow. But eventually. And finally.

Belief in the promise of ultimate victory should affect the way we live our lives in the present. An analogy might be helpful. Let's say we play on a football team. Our team, 2-8, is playing a crucial game against a formidable opponent, 10-0. Let's say that before the game our team learns—with absolute certainty—that we are going to win this game. For sure! No doubt about it!

How would such knowledge affect our playing? Some might say it would make us lethargic. "If we know we're going to win, why put forth any effort?" Possibly. But not probably. I think such knowledge would fire us up. It would increase our courage and self-confidence, thus enabling us to play better than ever perhaps.

But let's say, at the end of the first quarter we're down 14-0. Would we be discouraged? Not really. Knowledge of the final victory would help to keep us in the game. In fact, if at half-time we were down 31-0, we might find ourselves saying things like this: "Down by 31—yet we're going to win? Incredible! I can't wait to play the second half to see how we pull this one out!" Or, "Down by 31! We've gotta get some incredible breaks to turn this one around. Lady Luck's gotta start smiling on us! After all, we can't do it ourselves. We're not that good. We've shown that!"

And that's exactly true. In order to win we would need some breaks. Perhaps the opposing quarterback dislocates his shoulder and has to leave the game. Maybe their defense, overly confident because of their 31-point lead, starts to get sloppy and begins to make all kinds of fundamental mistakes. And maybe our kicker is aided by a favorable wind, the football takes a few crazy bounces in our favor, and our quarterback throws a successful Hail Mary pass in the end zone. Whatever, we play the game with energy and enthusiasm, using the limited skills we have, relying on other forces to help us, confident in the knowledge of ultimate victory, and what happens? We finally do win the game—in overtime—34–31. Ultimate victory!

In the game of life, Jesus promises us ultimate victory: life over death, goodness over evil, joy over sorrow. Maybe at this moment we don't feel close to victory. In fact, maybe we're down by 14 or even 31. But our belief in Jesus' promise keeps us in the game—to the end. We play with courage and enthusiasm, utilizing what limited skills we have, and trusting not in our own power, but in the power of Jesus who assures us that ultimate victory will be ours!

Jesus, strengthen my belief in your promise of ultimate victory, and may that belief affect the way I live this day.

❀ ❀ ❀

68) Temporary friendships

There's something in us that wants friendships to last forever. And miraculously, some do. Some friendships manage to weather the floods and droughts of everyday living, to negotiate the unexpected turns and hairpin curves of two separate lives—and last a lifetime. For these, we thank God.

But what about those other friendships that last for only a time? Those that gradually fade away or abruptly and painfully come to an end? Can we thank God for these, too?

I think we can. And should. For even temporary friendships bequeath to us memories and gifts that cannot be taken away from us even once the friendship has ended. Furthermore, just because a friendship ends doesn't mean it wasn't a blessing—at least for a certain period of our lives. Some friendships end because the two friends grow apart. These endings, as painful as they may be, call us to respect both ourselves and the other person, for we know we cannot continue in a relationship that does violence to either party. Some broken relationships remind us that the best thing we can say to some individuals is "goodbye." When we do this, we're acknowledging, in all humility, that our friendship is not meant for everyone.

The poet John Donne wrote, "No (one) is an island," but Anne Morrow Lindbergh disagreed when she wrote, "We are all islands in a common sea." Temporary friendships underscore the great truth of our basic "island-ness," our essential solitariness.

God, help me to reflect on some of the temporary friendships in my life and to thank you for them.

❧ ❧ ❧

69) Mary pondered

If there's one thing we know about Mary from the gospels, it is this: she liked to ponder things. When the angel Gabriel first appeared to her he said, "Greetings, favored one! The Lord is with you" (Lk 1:28). Mary was "much perplexed by his words and pondered what sort of greeting this might be" (Lk 1:29). Later, when the shepherds came to visit the newborn child, Mary is shown pondering once again: "She treasured all these words and pondered them in her heart" (Lk 2:19).

When Mary and Joseph presented Jesus in the temple, Simeon made a prophecy concerning the child. How did they react to his words? "The child's father and mother were amazed at what was being said about him" (Lk 2:33). In other words, they pondered Simeon's prophecy. Twelve years later, when Mary and Joseph found the lost Jesus in the temple, Luke says, "His mother treasured all these things in her heart" (Lk 2:51). She reflected on this event and her son's words to her. Years later on Calvary, John tells us that Mary was there, "standing near the cross" (Jn 19:25). Even as Jesus was dying, Mary continued to ponder the meaning of this seemingly catastrophic event.

What does all of this have to do with us? Like Mary, we are called to be ponderers too. We are called to reflect on the events of our lives, to weigh matters carefully before acting, to actively seek new meanings and new possibilities. Sometimes we will ponder in joy—for example, when we see a newborn baby, experience the support of a friend, or receive a consolation in prayer. At other times, we will ponder in sorrow—when we mourn the death of a loved one, behold all the evil in the world, or experience dryness in prayer.

For all of these times, Mary can be our model, for when it comes to pondering, she shows us the way.

Mary, teach me to ponder the events in my life, that I may see in them new meanings and new possibilities.

❦ ❦ ❦

70) Throwing bouquets

One of my college professors, Sister Mary St. Joseph, used to tell us in class: "Don't save your roses for people's funerals. Throw your bouquets to people while they're still alive!" What matters, she was saying, is what we give or say to individuals while they are still living, and not what we give (a fancy casket) or say about them ("What a wonderful man he was!") after they're dead.

Every time I attend a wake and listen to all the good things people say about the deceased, I am tempted to ask, "Did you say those things to her while she was still alive?" In many cases, the individuals have—thank God. But in some instances, they never did. Consequently, some people go to their graves without ever knowing how much they really meant to others, how much they were loved and admired by them. And if they had only known, what a difference that knowledge might have made in their lives. How much more pleasant, easier, and happier their earthly journey could have been.

Our bouquets need not be big or expensive. A simple word of praise, a small thank-you, a little pat on the back will do.

God, help me to throw a bouquet to someone today.

❧ ❧ ❧

71) Playing hide-and-seek with a squirrel

Yesterday I saw a squirrel out by the cemetery. As soon as he spotted me, he ran up a tree, stopping about five feet off the ground. Curious, I walked closer to that tree. As I did, the squirrel scooted around to the opposite side of the tree. Then I started to walk slowly around the tree. As I did, the squirrel went around the tree too, always keeping the tree between himself and me. I felt as if I were playing hide-and-seek with him. Just as I was determined to see that squirrel, so was he determined not to be seen by me!

Finally, I stopped and started going in the opposite direction. Sure enough, I caught the squirrel coming around the other way. When he spotted me, he flicked his tail and immediately reversed his direction. Around and around we went again for several more minutes.

Later, I thought: that's how I am with God at times. I'm like that little squirrel, living a life of caution and scurrying. Out of nowhere, God enters my world. I'm afraid (understandably so!), but curious enough (fortunately!) not to run completely away from God. Instead, I scurry up a nearby tree and cling to its solid trunk. When God comes closer, I begin to go around and around the tree, always careful to keep the tree—or some other barrier—between God and me. It's not that I'm terrified of God, mind you. If so, I'd run all the way up to the top of the tree. No, I'm fascinated by God, but also mistrustful enough not to let God get too close.

God, help me to name the barriers I keep between you and myself. And lead me to trust you more.

❧ ❧ ❧

72) Quotes on gratitude

Gratitude is the memory of the heart. (Greek proverb)

Feeling gratitude and not expressing it is like wrapping a present and not giving it. (William Arthur Ward)

If the only prayer you say in your whole life is "thank you," that would suffice. (Meister Eckhart)

No duty is more urgent than that of returning thanks. (St. Ambrose)

To stand on one's legs and prove God's existence is a very different thing from going on one's knees and thanking God. (Søren Kierkegaard)

Thank you, God. And help me to express my gratitude to others today.

❧ ❧ ❧

73) When it rains on our picnic

When I was a novice, my community sponsored its first chicken barbecue. Weeks before, we sent out flyers to family and friends. We nuns (especially us young ones) worked like crazy preparing for the big day. We washed dishes, sorted silverware, made jello, baked apple pies, set up tables outside, etc. And every evening, we prayed together in chapel: "May God give us good weather for the barbecue." With five hundred nuns praying for good weather, I was sure God would give us a nice, sunny day.

But I was wrong. Sunday morning we awoke to rain. Heavy rain. Continuous rain. That morning we frantically moved everything inside. We set up tables and chairs in parlors, classrooms, hallways, garages—wherever we could find space. And the people came— several hundred that first year. A few complained about parking on the soggy grass and eating in such cramped quarters, but the vast majority took the rain and mud in stride and enjoyed themselves. (They must have, for they came back the next year and the next. Today we serve over 5,000 chicken dinners at each barbecue!)

But that Sunday morning many years ago, when I saw all that rain, I said to God, "How could you let it rain?! And after we all prayed for good weather, too!" I wondered, was God mad at us? Had we done something wrong? Was God against barbecues?

The simple truth is, of course, that God does not always answer our prayers—at least not in the way we expect or want. We pray for sun, and it rains on our picnic. Or (more seriously) we pray that a loved one get well, and he or she dies. Sometimes we may eventually learn why we did not get what we asked for. But many times, we will never know why. The question is: do we trust God only because God answers our prayers the way we want, or do we trust God enough to accept any answer to our prayers that God may give?

God, teach me to ask you for things, but give me enough trust to accept any answer you may give.

❦ ❦ ❦

74) On giving scandal

If there is one thing Jesus was good at, it was giving scandal. He ate with sinners (Mt 9:9–13), cured on the sabbath (Mk 3:1–6), spoke openly with women on the street (Jn 4:1–42), and even allowed a lady of the night to invade his personal space in broad daylight (Lk 7:36–50). The scribes and Pharisees found such behavior scandalous, shocking, and (eventually) intolerable.

There is something about Jesus giving scandal that attracts me. When I read these accounts, I find myself cheering Jesus on. "You show 'em, Jesus!" I say. "Shock the heck out of them!"

Why do I react this way? It's not because I think scandal is, in itself, a good thing. No. Nor do I think Jesus' aim in these instances was solely to give scandal. On the contrary, Jesus' aim in all of these cases was simply this: to do the loving thing. In other words, his aim was to make God's love incarnate in this particular time and place, with these specific individuals. If doing that gave scandal to others, then so be it.

The old adage says, "Beauty is in the eye of the beholder." So is scandal. If we do not see reality with the eyes of Jesus, then we will be scandalized by his actions. But if we do see with Jesus' eyes, we will behold the beauty in everything he did.

God, help me to make your love incarnate in my time and place, with the individuals you put into my day. If doing this gives scandal to others, so be it.

❧ ❧ ❧

75) "Here I am, God"

Throughout scripture we find individuals saying to God, "Here I am." When God calls to Moses from the burning bush, Moses answers, "Here I am" (Ex 3:4). When God summons Samuel in the middle of the night, Samuel responds with, "Here I am" (1 Sm 3:4). And when God asks the prophet Isaiah, "Whom shall I send?" Isaiah replies, "Here am I; send me!" (Is 6:8).

Those three little words make a beautiful prayer. Here I am. Not there. Not where I used to be or where I will be someday or where I wish I were. But here. In this place. Amid these specific circumstances. Here I am. Not as I was yesterday or as I will be tomorrow or as I wish I were. But as I am. In this condition, this shape. With these particular thoughts and feelings.

Perhaps all prayer should begin with a simple, "Here I am, God." It should begin with the humble acknowledgment and acceptance of where we find ourselves and who we are on this particular day. Only then can we hope to begin to move forward and beyond—with God's grace, of course.

Here I am, God. With your grace, help me to begin to move beyond where and who I am today.

❦ ❦ ❦

76) Fallow time

Currently I live in Detroit, but since my family and religious community are both near Cleveland, I often drive between the two cities. Whenever I do, I am amazed at all the farmland I see en route, especially in northwestern Ohio. Literally miles and miles of flat fields stretch as far as the eye can see on both sides of the turnpike. In summer these fields are burgeoning with green crops— mostly corn and soybeans, I've noticed. But in the fall, after the crops have been harvested, these same fields are brown and bare, plowed up and lying fallow.

Seeing these fallow fields conjures up for me a line from Sue Bender's book *Everyday Sacred*: "We all need a certain amount of fallow time." Fallow. The word is rich and lovely. Strictly speaking, it describes land that has been plowed up but intentionally left unseeded, thus giving the land a chance to rest, to reclaim its nutrients.

We all need a certain amount of fallow time in our lives. We need times of rest and nonproductivity, times to reclaim our nutrients. In these fallow times we step out of our "doer mode" and slip into our "be-er mode." These are times we just stare out windows, watch clouds float by, listen to crickets chirping, play with a child, daydream. In short, we "waste" time.

What happens when we don't have fallow time in our lives? Bender tells us: "There is a deeper intelligence that won't come forth." That "deeper intelligence" is often, I suspect, the low, sweet voice of God whispering in our hearts.

God, help me to reclaim some fallow time both in my day and in my life.

❦ ❦ ❦

77) Keep laughing

Laughing is good for us on all levels: physical, psychological, social, and spiritual. If that is true, then sometimes the best thing for our general well being is a simple joke, like these:

- A pessimist is someone who looks both ways before crossing a one-way street.
- Question: How many paranoids does it take to change a light bulb? Answer: Why do you want to know?
- As I grow older, there are three things I have trouble remembering: faces, names, and…I can't remember what the third thing is.
- Tell me, how did you become so successful? Two words: right decisions. And how did you make right decisions? One word: experience. And how did you get experience? Two words: wrong decisions.
- Archives: where Noah kept his two bees.

Keep me laughing, God.

78) God's circus

In his book *Vital Spiritualities*, Gerard Broccolo uses the image of a circus to describe the church. The circus is a good image, he maintains, for that is what we, the church, really are: "a motley conglomerate of colors, movements, sounds, and smells." The modern-day parish, Broccolo says, is a three-ring or even ten-ring circus: "More is happening than anyone can control. Things often get done haphazardly. One thing is planned and another happens."

The image of the church as a circus is an apt one for other reasons, too. The life of the circus is one of complexity, humor, daring, magic, glitter, pathos. We laugh at the clowns, gasp at the tightrope walkers, and shudder at the sideshow freaks, knowing all along that we are somehow they, and they are somehow us. The circus never stays in one place for very long, either, but is always on the move to somewhere else.

The circus, like the church, is not perfect. It is guilty of gross inconsistencies, serious injustices, and downright foolishness at times. Yet, despite these obvious human limitations, the circus is ultimately meant to be enjoyed. Says Broccolo, if we love one another as Jesus loves us, we, the church, can finally enjoy each other in our differences and shortcomings, and "in our disjointed movements and disparate colors, sounds, and smells."

The church is a circus. Who knows? It just might be, after all, the greatest show on earth.

God, give me a greater acceptance of and love for your circus, the church.

❦ ❦ ❦

79) Haste makes sense

Benjamin Franklin said, "Haste makes waste." But scripture offers another view. It says that sometimes haste makes sense.

Concerning the first Passover meal, God gives these directives to the Israelites, "You shall eat it hurriedly" (Ex 12:11). After all, if our life is in danger, we'd better not dilly-dally. Throughout the psalms, we find this prayer addressed to God: "Make haste to help me" (Ps 38:22). When it comes to getting help from God, don't we all want immediate results?

After the Annunciation, Mary goes "with haste to a Judean town in the hill country" (Lk 1:39) to visit her cousin Elizabeth. Joy and excitement have a way of propelling us—even over the hills in life. After Jesus' birth, the shepherds go "with haste" (Lk 2:16) to find the newborn king. When our destination is love incarnate, why would we ever drag our feet? Even Jesus himself encouraged haste. When he spots Zacchaeus in that sycamore tree, Jesus calls, "Zacchaeus, hurry and come down; for I must stay at your house today" (Lk 19:5). Zacchaeus scrambles down from that tree, for, if we have received an invitation from Jesus himself, we hustle.

The truth is, of course, we don't have all the time in the world. Therefore, sometimes we must make haste: when we are fleeing danger, asking for God's help, brimming with joy and excitement, seeking love incarnate, and responding to an invitation from Jesus himself. At such times, haste makes sense. The only sense.

God, make haste to help me. And may I also make haste to help others today.

❦ ❦ ❦

80) Jealousy and our intrinsic ache for "the more"

Jealousy is an ugly beast. Whenever it rears its hideous head above the waterline of my subconscious, I get anxious. "Down, Jealousy, down!" I whisper nervously. "Down before somebody sees you!

Down before I have to deal with you!"

When I find myself jealous of someone else's talents and good fortune, I am embarrassed. I feel small and ungrateful. "Why should you be jealous," I say to myself sternly, "when you've received so many blessings—your family, friends, health, talents? Why can't you just be satisfied?!"

Be satisfied? That's the word that helped me see jealousy in a more positive light. Yes, jealousy can be an ugly thing when it blinds us to our own gifts, or when it goads us into wishing or inflicting harm upon another. But jealousy can also be a benevolent thing when it reminds us that we will never be completely satisfied here on earth, no matter how gifted or successful we are, no matter how much love we give and receive. We'll always feel this longing for more. In fact, when we're jealous of others, it's usually because we assume they possess "the more" we're missing—more talent, more money, more power, more freedom, more love. And, if only we had what they have, we'd never be jealous again. Ha!

Yes, jealousy can be an ugly beast. But it can also be a friendly little imp who keeps popping up to remind us of our intrinsic ache for "the more," which ultimately, of course, is God.

God, you alone can satisfy my deepest longings. Help me to befriend my intrinsic ache for "the more."

❦ ❦ ❦

81) The prodigality of the pear trees

Today I bit into a fresh, ripe pear and *presto*! I was instantly transported back in time (over forty years) and space (over 220 miles) to our small farm in northeastern Ohio, a farm that doesn't even exist anymore. My right brain did the transporting—instantaneously—leaving my poor left brain scrambling to figure out how

I had done it. It kept reasoning, "How could we be in Detroit, Michigan one minute and in Willoughby Hills, Ohio the next? And how come it's not today anymore but suddenly 1956?"

Only after a few seconds did my left brain figure it out. "I've got it! It was the taste of that pear!" it concluded excitedly. And it was right. For the pear I had bitten into tasted exactly like the pears we used to have on our farm years ago, pears that were strewn all over our yard in late summer. To my recollection, they all came from five pear trees: three small ones on the side of the house and two very tall ones by the end of the driveway. Every year these five trees provided us with an abundance of pears, even though we never actually cultivated those trees or sprayed them. In fact, we all but ignored them all year long—except in the spring when we admired their blossoms, and in the fall when we ate their fruit.

Sometimes in life, we toil long and hard to produce good fruit: a strong marriage, decent kids, an effective ministry. But other times, the fruit just happens with little or no effort on our part. Or as scripture says, "A good measure, pressed down, shaken together, running over, will be put into your lap" (Lk 6:38). Ker-plunk! Just like that!

Biting into that pear today led me to give thanks for all of life's gratuitous fruits.

Thank you, God, for all the fruits you've given me out of your prodigality.

❄ ❄ ❄

82) The little girl with the yellow bow

Sometimes I pray with pictures. One of the pictures I've used is that of a dark-haired little girl about five years old. She is a refugee living in a makeshift camp in some war-torn part of the world. The specifics are not important. What is important is that she is a real child. What's more, she's thin, she's wearing a muddy, red dress, and she's staring at the camera with fear and apprehension. But what strikes me most about the picture is what is perched on top of the little girl's head: a big yellow bow.

Who put it there? I wonder. Certainly not the little girl, for when I look closer I see that the bow is partly braided into her hair. Someone else had to have put it there. Her mother perhaps? Does she even have a mother? And I wonder: amid such transience and squalor, how does anyone manage to find—let alone hang on to—a yellow bow?

Other questions arise effortlessly: what is the little girl's name? What horrors has she seen and experienced already in her young life? Does she play with any toys? Does she even know how to play? Is anyone teaching her to read and write?

The yellow bow is the only sign of hope I have for this little girl. I reassure myself: "Somebody is caring for this child. See? They fixed a bow in her hair." Yes, somebody is caring for her. Then I add soberly, "But against what odds?"

The picture reminds me of something I read once: "There can be no real joy for anybody until there is joy finally for all of us." I agree completely. As long as there is one child like this little girl anywhere in the world, we cannot be fully joyful.

God, please help us to watch over all of the world's children. And help me to watch over the ones you put into my life.

❧ ❧ ❧

83) Ministry: punishment or privilege?

After teaching four years at Notre Dame College in Cleveland, Ohio, I was transferred to Cardinal Gibbons High School in Raleigh, North Carolina. Here I taught religion and English to seniors. I had been at Gibbons only a week or two, when a senior boy asked at the beginning of class, "Sister, is it true that you taught college before coming here?"

"Yes, I did," I answered.

What the boy asked next, I will never forget: "Then being sent here to teach us—was that some kind of a punishment?"

I had to smile at his question—in a way. But in another way, I couldn't, for the boy was completely serious. He was assuming that being sent to Gibbons to teach him and his classmates was some kind of a step down for me.

I assured the boy that coming to Raleigh was not a demotion. And teaching him and his classmates was certainly no punishment. "In fact," I said, "Being here with you is a privilege." And I meant those words.

We spend our lives doing all kinds of work and ministry: we raise families, administer parishes, teach CCD, volunteer at soup kitchens. What kind of message do we send to the people we serve? Being here with you is a punishment? Or, being here with you is a privilege?

God, help me to communicate this message to the people I serve: being here with you is a privilege!

❧ ❧ ❧

84) Experiencing pleasure

St. John of Damascus (c. 675–c. 749) taught that the primary purpose of sexual intercourse was pleasure. (Upon hearing that, one of my colleagues remarked, "One wonders how this teaching, over the years, got shuffled to the bottom of the deck!")

Sometimes religious people tend to view pleasure, whether sexual or otherwise, with displeasure, if you will, or with mistrust or even antagonism. We are more apt to associate pleasure with sin than with sanctity. And that's unfortunate. For scripture tells us over and over again that God is someone who experiences pleasure. "The Lord takes pleasure...in those who hope in his steadfast love" (Ps 147:11). "The Lord takes pleasure in his people" (Ps 149:4). Even Jesus himself described a God who was no stranger to pleasure: "It is your Father's good pleasure to give you the kingdom" (Lk 12:32). Jesus himself was labeled a glutton (Mt 11:19), simply because he took pleasure in tasty food and fine wine.

Pleasure, then, is never bad in itself. On the contrary, it is one of the ways we encounter the divine in the everyday. Simple pleasures (the scent of pine, the feel of a kitten's fur, the song of a wren, the taste of a strawberry, the embrace of a loved one) can bring us closer to God. Enjoying them now prepares us for the fullness of God's presence where there will be "pleasures forevermore" (Ps 16:11).

God, come to me in the pleasures of this day.

❧ ❧ ❧

85) "Give this matter the attention it deserves"

When Rome sends a letter to the bishops of the world, it often concludes with, "Give this matter the attention it deserves." Rome is assuming, I imagine, that all of its matters are of great importance and deserving of serious attention. But I suspect on more than one occasion, there's a bishop somewhere who judges otherwise. "Give this matter the attention it deserves?" he says to himself. "Okay," and he slips the letter underneath the stack of other letters already piled on his desk.

The directive "Give this matter the attention it deserves" has become something of a watchword for me. When some petty thing begins to bother me, I say to myself, "Give this matter the attention it deserves." Translation? "Forget it! It doesn't deserve the attention you're giving it!" Or when some inconsequential task begins to usurp too much of my valuable time and energy, I remind myself, "Give this matter the attention it deserves." In other words, "Let go of it already! It's not worth it!"

Sometimes the opposite happens, and I want to rush through an important job. I remind myself, "Slow down! Give this task the attention it deserves." I have no time to visit a friend or play with a child? I tell myself, "Stop and give them the attention they deserve!"

A grace to pray for: to be able to give all things the attention they truly deserve.

God, help me to give things the attention they deserve today.

❧ ❧ ❧

86) Humility and the illusion of personal autonomy

In his book *Cherish Christ Above All*, Demetrius Dumm, OSB, says this about humility: "To be humble is to be realistic about what one can or cannot achieve by personal effort. It is opposed, not to self-esteem, but to the illusion of personal autonomy."

Too often in the past we have thought of humility in terms of self-abasement: "I'm nobody...I can't do anything...I'm no good." How much more accurate it is to view humility in terms of our intrinsic need for others: "I can't go it alone...I have to have help with this...I need God."

"The illusion of personal autonomy...." Maybe that's the form pride most often takes in our day. Pride: when we deify control and autonomy. Pride: when we assume our achievements are the sole result of our personal effort. Pride: when we reject the assistance of friend, ally, community, and even God.

God, enable me to be realistic about what I can or cannot achieve by personal effort. In other words, keep me humble.

❧ ❧ ❧

87) Putting the groceries away

There are essentially two attitudes toward putting the groceries away: attitude A and attitude B.

A: These bags weigh a ton. I hate carrying groceries into the house.

B: How lucky I am to have all these bags of groceries to carry into my house.

A: Humpf! Bananas went up three cents a pound!

B: Thank you, God, for giving me bananas in November—and oranges, and apples, and lettuce, too.

A: I hate this freezer! It's so small, I can hardly fit these frozen vegetables in!

B: How lucky am I to own a freezer when most of the world's peoples have never even seen one, let alone own one!

A: That stupid store was out of butter pecan frozen yogurt, so I had to settle for pralines and cream.

B: I'm amazed at the variety of flavors we have in frozen yogurt these days! With so many, it's hard to decide which one to buy.

A: I can't believe I was charged for four cans of soup when I bought only three! What an injustice!

B: So the store charged me for a can of soup I didn't buy. I'll call it to their attention next week—probably. What kind of an injustice is that compared to the kind that deprives millions of people of all food—including even soup?

A: There! I'm finally finished putting all those groceries away. I'm glad that job's over with!

B: There! I'm finished putting all my groceries away. How blessed I am!

Thank you, God, for all the food I have in my house. Help me to be mindful of those who have little or no food in their house—if they have a house.

❧ ❧ ❧

88) God likes spunk

Scripture tells us that God likes submission. "Submit yourselves therefore to God," St. James tells us (Jas 4:7). "Yield yourselves to God," echoes St. Paul (Rom 6:13). And the prophet Samuel makes clear, "To obey is better than sacrifice" (1 Sm 15:22).

Submit. Yield. Obey. Yes, God likes submission. But does God also like spunk? Does God like pluck? I think so. All we have to do is look at Jesus.

Jesus appreciated submission. He appreciated the submission of a Roman centurion (Lk 7:1–10), of the blind Bartimaeus (Mk 10:46–52), of the repentant woman (Lk 7:36–50). But he also appreciated spunk; he also welcomed pluck.

Take, for instance, the story of the Syrophoenician woman (Mk 7:24–30). She comes to Jesus, bows submissively at his feet, and begs him to cure her daughter who was possessed by a demon. She's a Gentile, a non-Jew. Jesus at first seems to refuse her request. "It is not fair to take the children's food and throw it to the dogs," he says. Despite the apparent insult, the woman persists. With incredible spunk (not to mention creativity) she replies, "Sir, even the dogs under the table eat the children's crumbs." Her clever retort wins Jesus over. He says to her (probably with a grin), "For

saying that, you may go—the demon has left your daughter."
Submission is appreciated, yes, but spunk is rewarded!

Our prayer doesn't always have to be, "Thy will be done,
Lord...Whatever you say...You know what's best, God." Sometimes
God expects and even appreciates it when we fling God's way a few
No's!, Darn's!, Hell's!, and even Damn it's!.

God, give me spunk!

❧ ❧ ❧

89) "It's okay to have a crabby day"

In his book *Spiritual Surrender*, Jim Krisher relates how, during the
early weeks of his marriage, he was having a bad day. For no apparent reason he was sullen and irritable. At the end of the day, he
apologized profusely to his wife for his behavior. She simply
smiled and said, "It's okay to have a crabby day."

St. Paul says, "God loves a cheerful giver" (2 Cor 9:7). That's
true. But it doesn't mean that God expects us to be a cheerful giver
24 hours a day, 365 days out of the year! God is far too much of a
realist to demand that, and far too much of a friend. In fact, God
would be the first to say to us, "It's okay to have a crabby day." God
would also say: It's okay to get tired...It's okay to be sad...It's okay
to doubt...It's okay to let your guard down. In other words, it's
okay to be human.

*God, my friend, let me hear you say to me today, "It's okay
to be human."*

❧ ❧ ❧

90) The tyranny of personal preference

When I taught high school, sometimes my religion class would have a Mass together, and I would recruit a few kids to plan the liturgy. Inevitably, after looking over the readings for the day, one would ask, "Do we have to use the readings of the day—or can we pick the ones we want?" Almost always, I would answer, "Let's use the readings already chosen for this day." My reply usually elicited a groan or two, and one kid would sometimes say, "But we don't like those readings! Why can't we pick ones we like?"

Fair question. Depending on how much time I had, I would explain to my students that sticking only to scripture we liked was not wise. If we kept choosing only passages that appealed to us, we were selling ourselves short. Scripture is meant to console us, yes. And it usually does that when we hear our favorite passages—like the parable of the prodigal son, for example. But scripture is also meant to challenge us and, on occasion, even to disturb us. This is more likely to happen when we read passages we don't like, passages which, given the choice, we would prefer to avoid—for example, the parable of the Last Judgment.

We live in an age that glorifies personal preference. "Have it your way," could well be the watchword of our times. Parents run up against this all the time. They know there are times they can give in to their children's preferences: "What kind of cake would you like for your birthday?" But parents also know, there are times they ignore or even go against the preferences of their children: "No, you can't stay home from school today." "You must eat your vegetables!"

Someone once used the expression "the tyranny of personal preference." It's an apt phrase, for if we allow our personal preferences to govern our lives, we will not be free to move beyond where or who we are. Instead, we will be stuck in our own little world—a world cozy and safe, yes, but a world pale and impoverished.

God, move me beyond my personal preferences today.

Everything that seems empty is full
of the angels of God.

— *St. Hilary*

WINTER

91) "The conviction of things not seen"

A man boarded a plane with his son and his son's friend, both of whom were priests. The man sat in the middle seat, a little apprehensive at the prospect of flying. Detecting his fear before take off, the flight attendant reassured him cheerfully, "You've got nothing to worry about, sitting between two priests." The man was skeptical. "What do you think priests are?" he asked. "Propellers?"

This humorous anecdote illustrates something serious about faith: faith asks us to trust in things not seen when we'd naturally prefer something much more visible and concrete—like propellers!

In the letter to the Hebrews we read: "Faith is the assurance of things hoped for, the conviction of things not seen" (Heb 11:1). Faith asks us to believe in things that are very real, but not necessarily always clearly visible. What things? The goodness in people, the power of love, the beauty in the ordinary, the presence of God.

God, strengthen my faith today. Give me the assurance of things hoped for, the conviction of things not seen.

∾∾∾

92) One sentence at a time

Sometimes people ask me, "How do you write all those books?" I reply, "One sentence at a time." I'm not being facetious. I'm just being accurate. That's how anyone writes a book. Similarly, that's how anyone writes a symphony: one note at a time; how anyone builds a building: one brick at a time; and how anyone runs a marathon: one step at a time.

There's a certain wisdom in breaking life down into more manageable pieces. Otherwise we risk being overwhelmed by what lies before us. For years I kept churning out articles—literally hundreds of them—but the idea of writing a book seemed beyond my capabilities. Then one day, a friend of mine, Sister Kathleen Glavich, herself the author of several books, said to me, "Don't think of it as writing a book, Melannie. Think of it as writing a bunch of articles!" The idea of writing a few dozen more articles didn't intimidate me, so I set out to do it. The result? *Peeling Back Eggshells*, my first book or (if you prefer) my first collection of forty-five short articles!

All recovering alcoholics subscribe to a similar philosophy. They do not endeavor to abstain from alcohol for the rest of their lives, but only for today. They know: string together enough todays, and you have a lifetime!

Jesus advocated a similar wisdom when he instructed us to ask God for our daily bread (Mt 6:11). Live your life one day at a time, he was implying.

God, help me to break my life down into more manageable pieces. Teach me to live my life one day at a time.

93) Befriending darkness

When Thomas Edison invented the light bulb, he gave us a marvelous gift. But, as with all gifts, the light bulb has its downside: it has given us a lack of appreciation for or even a mistrust of darkness.

Think of it: prior to light bulbs, people spent a great part of their lives in the dark—or nearly dark. Candles, kerosene lamps, and gas lights were precious commodities used sparingly. When it got dark, most people either sat in the dark or went to bed. What a contrast to us who just flick on a light and continue to do whatever we were already doing before it got dark. No longer needing to restrict our activities to daylight hours, we have the "luxury" of working twenty-four hours a day if we choose.

John Staudenmaier, SJ, at the University of Detroit Mercy, has written and lectured extensively on both the positive and negative influences of modern technology on humanity. He sometimes invites people to abstain from technology for twenty-four hours. If that's not possible, he encourages people at least to do without light bulbs for a day or so. His purpose? To enable people to appreciate the beauty, power, and mystery of darkness, to help them see darkness not merely as the absence of light, but as a wonderfully beautiful entity in and of itself. Some things, for example, occur only in darkness: the sprouting of a seed, the development of an unborn child, the bustle of nocturnal animals and insects. We humans know the beauty of eating by candlelight, sitting around a campfire, praying in an unlit chapel, making love in the darkness.

God loves light, it's true, but God loves darkness as well. In fact, it is precisely in darkness that God spoke to Moses: "Then the people stood at a distance, while Moses drew near to the darkness where God was" (Ex 20:21). At the dedication of the Temple, King Solomon says to the people: "The Lord said he would dwell in thick darkness" (1 Kgs 8:12). And the psalmist says of God: "He made darkness his covering around him" (Ps 18:11).

Maybe we would do well to accept John Staudenmaier's invitation to do without light bulbs for a day or two. Who knows, we might not only befriend darkness, we might even encounter God.

God, help me to befriend the darkness.

❧❧❧

94) "You are a doe"

It was one of those faculty in-service days in the 1970s. We were paired off to get to know each other better by sharing our thoughts and feelings one-on-one. The question was asked: "What animal does your fellow faculty member remind you of—and why?" Most of us proceeded to answer the question with caution. Understandably so. No one wants to tell someone he's a rhino or she's a porcupine.

I was paired up with a male colleague. When it was his turn to tell me what animal I reminded him of, he said without hesitation, "You are a doe." And he went on to explain why. I remember being very flattered and encouraged. His remark made a deep impression on me, for here it is, so many years later, and I can still remember his words and the image it conjured up for me.

"You are a doe." The incident reminded me of the great power we have to influence (for better or for worse) the concept others have of themselves. For better: "You're great!" For worse: "You're stupid!" And how enduring is the power of an image: "You're an angel!" or "You're a jerk!"

Jesus used images to bolster the self-esteem of others. He called the rambunctious Peter a "rock" (Mt 16:18). He labeled the bent-over woman "a daughter of Abraham" (Lk 13:16). He addressed his followers as "little flock" (Lk 12:32). And on the night before he died, he called his disciples, "friends" (Jn 15:14).

A good question to ask ourselves periodically: what images of themselves am I communicating to others by how I address and relate to them?

God, help me to bolster the self-esteem of others by how I address and relate to them.

√√√

95) Quotes on wisdom

All human wisdom is summed up in two words: wait and hope. (Alexandre Dumas)

Taking things apart is the result of knowledge; wisdom is putting them back together again. (Anonymous)

Wisdom consists not so much in knowing what to do in the ultimate as in knowing what to do next. (Herbert Hoover)

Not until you have the courage to meet yourself face to face will you have taken the first step along the path of wisdom. (Anonymous)

There is little room for wisdom when one is full of judgment. (Malcolm Hein)

God, give me wisdom!

96) The silver chalice: a sacred trust

I was making a three-day retreat at the Jesuit retreat center near Detroit. Before Mass, the celebrant told us we would be using the chalice that, in all likelihood, belonged to the Jesuit priest Jacques Marquette, who ministered to Native Americans in Michigan in the seventeenth century. Then he told us the story of how the chalice was found.

In 1912, Father Dunigan, a diocesan priest, was missioned to Michigan's upper peninsula. One day two elderly Native American men came to his Mass. They sat in the back of the small church and gazed at him attentively. After doing this for several days, the two men accosted the priest after Mass and asked if he belonged to the same church that the blackrobes belonged to many years ago. When he said, "Yes," the men said, "Then we have something to give you."

The men led the priest into the woods where they stopped at the foot of a giant cypress tree. One of the men began digging in the ground until he unearthed a wooden box. Inside the decaying box was a chalice—blackened with tarnish, but pure silver. The inscription indicated it was, in all probability, Father Marquette's.

The men told Father Dunigan that many years ago a blackrobe served their people. When he had to leave, he entrusted the chalice to their tribe with the directive, "Give this to another blackrobe someday." For 250 years the Native American tribe had carefully guarded this treasure, passing on the secret of its hiding place from one generation to the next. When Father Dunigan appeared, the men felt it was time to hand over the chalice to this new blackrobe.

Dunigan described how he felt when the men placed the chalice into his hands: "Overcome with emotion, holding the sacred cup in trembling hands, I made a little speech of acceptance to the Indians, and thanked them in the name of Holy Mother the Church for so nobly acquitting themselves of so sacred a trust."

As I drank from that chalice at Mass that day, I too was filled with emotion as I held the sacred cup in trembling hands.

The story of Father Marquette's chalice is, in miniature, the story of our Christian faith. For our faith, too, is a treasure of incomparable worth passed down from one generation to the next, a treasure with which we are now entrusted.

God, I thank you for all my ancestors in the faith. May I, like them, prove a worthy custodian of so valuable a treasure.

⨗⨗⨗

97) The inner child

When I was a little girl, I felt sorry for grownups. At our family get-togethers, we kids had fun playing hide-and-seek in the corn field or swinging from trees in the backyard, while all the grownups did was sit around on lawn chairs and talk. Just talk! At age five, I couldn't imagine anything more boring, more "unfun."

Today when I'm at meetings, I sometimes think about being a kid again. As I sit around a table with six or so other serious adults having a serious discussion about some serious matter, I suddenly think: what if all of us sitting here now were suddenly five years old again? What changes would that make at this meeting? It's easy and fun to picture some of those changes: All of the men with hair, for example. All the women with pigtails or pony tails. All of us in play suits or rompers, giggling, squirming, laughing, shoving, poking. Needless to say, if we really were all five again, the meeting would probably end abruptly as we all decided (spontaneously and unanimously) to go outside and play!

We read much today about getting in touch with our "inner child." Jesus himself said, "Unless you change and become like children, you will never enter the kingdom of heaven" (Mt 18:3). It might serve us well, then, to get in touch not only with our own inner child, but also with the inner child of those around us—to view others not as complicated, conniving, and completed adults, but as good-willed, guileless, and growing children. Trusting that everyone does, indeed, possess an inner child (much like our own) could do wonders for improving relationships—not to mention expediting meetings.

Jesus, help me to be in touch with my own inner child and the inner child of the individuals you put into my life today.

⚭⚭⚭

98) Look again

All artists invite us to look again. The poet William Wordsworth invites us to look again at that host of yellow daffodils bobbing in the breeze. The sculptor Michelangelo asks us, "Do you really think you understand the meaning of the crucifixion? Well, look again!" and he places before us his magnificent Pietà for our contemplation. The painter Georgia O'Keeffe says, "You think a red poppy is only a red poppy? Then look again—at mine!"

Jesus, too, invites us to look again. He calls us to look again at our supposed enemy and see a man filled with compassion (Lk 10:25–37). He invites us to look again at an apparently worthless woman and see instead a lady of immense love (Mk 14:3-9). He dares us to gaze upon bread and wine and behold his body and blood (Lk 22:17-20). And he challenges us to look again at suffering and death and to detect in them joy and new life.

Writer John Stewart Collis wrote, "Faith is reborn whenever anyone chooses to take a good look at anything—even a potato." At what individuals or circumstances in my life might Jesus be inviting me to look again?

Jesus, teach me to look again.

99) Gesture as prayer

Throughout the ages, spiritual writers have maintained that posture and gesture are important components of prayer. Kneeling, for example, is a traditional posture of submission and can call to mind God's sovereignty. Genuflecting and bowing are gestures of reverence and can make us more aware of God's majesty. Closing our eyes can help us to focus better during prayer, while sitting quietly with opened hands on our lap can actually encourage our receptivity to God's word.

Bodily gestures do more, however, than merely aid us in prayer. Sometimes they themselves can actually become our prayer. Rabbi Abraham Heschel once said, "When I marched with Martin Luther King in Selma, I felt my legs were praying." How insightful! Ordinary physical movement becoming prayer! In a way, then, our body prays every time it is engaged in loving acts. What kinds of acts? Here are but a few:

Washing the dishes...shoveling snow...pouring coffee at a soup kitchen...addressing Christmas cards...filling a birdfeeder...rocking a cranky baby...watering plants...making love with one's spouse…offering an arm to an elderly friend…giving someone a back rub.

God, may I become more aware of my body praying today.

100) Befriending the older and the younger

Studies show that most of the friends we make during life are close to us in age. In fact, one study reported that most best friends are usually within eight years of each other. It's easy to see why. We start off in life doing many things according to age—like going to school, making our First Communion, playing sports. Even after we're out of school many of us still gravitate toward people who share a common history with us: "You remember Fibber McGee and Molly (or Howdy Doody, or the Brady Bunch, or whoever)? So do I!"

But our life is impoverished if we befriend only individuals around our age. For individuals older than we are have a wealth of history and experience beyond our own to share with us. Likewise, those much younger also have a wealth of history and experience beyond our own to share with us.

I have always admired the friendship of Teresa of Avila and John of the Cross, two great saints of the church. I remember how surprised I was, however, when I learned that Teresa was twenty-seven years older than John.

Surely, one of the best ways to broaden our perspective on life is to befriend someone significantly older or younger than ourselves.

God, help me to befriend someone outside my age bracket.

101) "Come, Lord Jesus!"

Advent is the season for longing. But what exactly are we longing for? The answer to that question can be found in the refrain used throughout Advent: "Come, Lord Jesus!" (Rv 22:20). Essentially, we are longing for the coming of Jesus: into our personal lives— our families, parishes, workplaces—into our local communities, and finally, into our nation and world.

With the means of communication available to us today, we are only too aware of those places where Jesus seems to be absent. Perhaps we ourselves are struggling with our own compulsions or are at odds with someone in our family. Or maybe we realize that the poor in our midst are being overlooked by our parish or local community. In addition, we get daily reports of violence and injustices in places all over the globe, places too numerous, unfortunately, even to keep track of. This painful awareness of Jesus' apparent absence can serve to intensify our longing for his coming.

Little wonder, then, that the season of Advent appeals to so many people. Its underlying refrain, "Come, Lord Jesus!" is the fundamental cry of our restless and anxious hearts.

Come, Lord Jesus!

❧❧❧

102) The Song of Songs

When I was a novice, I remember reading the Song of Songs and blushing. All that stuff about lips, breasts, navels and thighs made me wonder, "How did this book ever get into the Bible?!" I don't know how the Song of Songs ever made it into the Bible (I do know there was considerable controversy surrounding its inclusion). But I know one thing for sure now: I'm glad it's in!

Why? For one thing, the book is a magnificent celebration of the beauty of sexual love. And anyone who knows the history of the church knows it could use a little celebrating of erotic love. But I like the Song of Songs for yet another reason. It proclaims, in unforgettably beautiful and explicitly sensual language, that God longs for us. Just think of it: God longs for us. The Song of Songs makes clear what type of longing we're talking about, too. It's not the type of longing that has God saying, "I kinda like you." (Here insert a hearty handshake.) No, it's the kind of longing that a lover has for a "lovee." The kind that has God saying, "I desire you! I yearn for you! I want you! Come here!" (And here insert a lover's embrace.)

We are sometimes perceptive enough to realize our longing for God. But how often are we cognizant of God's passionate longing for us? Some lines from the Song of Songs might help us to contemplate this amazing reality. Imagine that God is saying these words to you:

"Let me see your face, let me hear your voice....Ah, you are beautiful, my love! Ah, you are beautiful, my beloved! Truly lovely! How sweet is your love! How much better is your love than wine! You are altogether beautiful, my love! Come, my beloved! Let us go forth into the fields....There I will give you my love!"

God, help me to feel your longing for me today.

∽∽∽

103) A world without animals

Recently a friend said to me, "I can't imagine a world without animals." She said this as she scratched the head of her golden retriever. I agreed with her as I tried to envision a world without animals. Just think of it: no dogs, cats, horses, squirrels, giraffes, goldfish, robins, elephants, whales. What an empty world it would be!

My friend's remark led me to reflect on other things I couldn't imagine living without: children, music, color, the sun, water, stories, touch, elderly people, mountains, stars, apples, friendship, imagination, prayer. Envisioning a world without these things only increased my appreciation for them. I ended up telling God what each of these gifts meant to me personally and thanking God for them.

What can't you imagine a world without? Why?

Thank you, God, for your many gifts that enrich our world, especially for _____.

ঔ ঔ ঔ

104) Mary as intercessor

These days we don't read too much about Mary as intercessor, let alone Mary as mediatrix of all graces. This is understandable. After all, scripture makes it clear that all salvation comes through Jesus. Peter proclaimed as much at the council of Jerusalem: "There is salvation in no one else, for there is no other name under heaven given among mortals by which we must be saved" (Acts 4:12).

The teaching that Mary is our intercessor with Jesus sometimes led people to conclude (falsely, of course) that salvation itself came from Mary and not from Jesus. Hence, our current confusion over Mary's precise role in salvation. I'm not about to clarify that role here. All I want to say is this: I, like Jesus, have a mother. Quite a wonderful one at that. And having her makes it easy for me to believe that Mary's role in salvation has to be more than a passive one. She is more than merely a vessel that housed the Son of God.

(Digression: Remember the song with the line "Mary, the shrine; Christ the God adored"? As novices, we used to giggle when we came to the line "Mary the grape, Christ the sacred wine." All we could picture was Mary as a big, fat, purple grape! Little inspiration for us in that line of poetry!)

But getting back to my mother…she doesn't call me very often. (I usually call her.) But when she does, it's usually to ask me for something. More often than not, it's a request for prayers for someone she's worried about. "Honey, Mrs. So-and-so just died. Could you please pray for her and her family?" Or "Uncle X is ill" or "Mr. Y just lost his job." Sometimes it's a material favor she's after: "How about sending Fr. Z a free copy of your new book?" I, for one, find it hard to refuse a mother's request.

From a theological point of view, Mary as intercessor may not make complete sense. But from a human point of view, it makes considerable sense—at least to me. And I imagine there's a young married couple from Cana that would agree with me (Jn 2:1–11).

Mary, help me to follow the directive you gave at Cana, "Do whatever my son tells you."

✠✠✠

105) Button up your overcoat

There's an old song that sometimes gets played during the cold winter months. It's called, "Button Up Your Overcoat." There's a line in that song that really speaks to me: "Take good care of yourself, you belong to me." The line expresses a fundamental truth about value and worth. Sometimes things are valuable and, hence, should be taken care of, simply because of the person to whom they belong. A ridiculous example of this is the garbage of famous people. Some individuals actually go through such garbage looking for items they might be able to sell: this famous actor's coffee grounds, that famous athlete's empty milk cartons. Ridiculous!

More worthy examples would be things like these: our grandmother's brooch, our father's high school ring, the quilt made by our great-aunt Tilly. These items themselves might not be worth that much on the open market. But because of the person to whom they belonged, they are priceless in our eyes.

When I was teaching, I sometimes struggled with seeing the worth of some students—especially when they were ornery or downright nasty. That's one reason I looked forward to meeting their parents or guardians—the people they belonged to. Such encounters often made me appreciate just how valuable each student was. I'd say to myself, "Remember: Jason is Jack and Karen's son," or "Heather is Ethel's granddaughter." Knowing that these parents and guardians were entrusting their most precious possession to me helped me to view my students in a more favorable light.

And if that didn't work for me, then I always fell back onto this incontrovertible truth: everyone is of value because everyone belongs to God.

God, help me to believe I belong to you—and so does everyone else I meet today.

∾∾∾

106) The need to please

There was a period in my life when I felt that ninety percent of my energy was going into trying to please everybody. It was as if all Ten Commandments had been reduced to one for me: "Thou shalt not displease thy neighbor." What brought me to this point in my life I'm not sure, but I have come up with a couple of contributing culprits.

First of all, I'm a woman. And even though recent years have seen significant strides in raising little girls and little boys with greater equality, most little girls of my generation were largely programmed to be "sugar and spice," that is, to be pleasing and nice. "Put your knees together like a good girl." "Don't bite your nails. It's not nice." "You've got to invite Roberta to your pajama party or you'll hurt her feelings." "Don't forget to write that thank-you note to Grandma. She'll be so pleased."

And if being a woman wasn't enough, I eventually became a nun—and everyone knows nuns were expected to be pleasing and nice all the time. We were supposed to please everyone—our sisters, superiors, students, pastors, and (of course) God. If we ever slipped up and displeased or hurt anyone, we promptly asked for a penance.

Trying to please everybody is a terrible way to live, for to achieve such a goal is downright impossible. By saying this, I am not advocating insensitivity to others. Heavens, no! I think I've written enough about the importance of sensitivity in life not to be accused of being insensitive to sensitivity! What I am saying is this: 1) Just because someone is hurt or displeased by what I say or do does not mean I am guilty of something. Sometimes I will hurt or displease others simply by being who I am, by making perfectly good and valid choices, and by speaking the truth that needs to be spoken. And 2) if I do hurt or displease someone and I rightly feel some guilt for what I've said or done, then Jesus advocated a wonderful energy-saving device to use in such instances: just say, "I'm sorry."

God, free me from my need to please everybody. And help me know when to say "I'm sorry."

∞∞∞

107) Humorous observations

Admiration is our polite recognition of another's resemblance to ourselves. (Anonymous)

Why is it that a twenty dollar bill looks so large in the collection basket in church and so small in the grocery store? (Anonymous)

Someone suggested this reponse to "Have a nice day": "Thank you, but I have other plans." (Paul Fussell)

A successful politician is someone who can stand on a fence and make people believe it's a platform. (Anonymous)

Television is an invention whereby you can be entertained in your living room by people you wouldn't have in your house. (David Frost)

Analyzing humor is like dissecting a frog. Few people are interested and the frog dies. (E. B. White)

Keep me laughing, God.

108) Criticism: speaking the truth in love

Someone once asked Cardinal Krol of Philadelphia who his spiritual advisor was. The Cardinal replied, "Just about everyone in the archdiocese!" The truth is, most of us will never lack for advisors or critics. All we have to do is say or do something, and they are sure to appear.

For some of us, criticism is hard to accept. Franklin Jones probably summed up how many of us feel about receiving criticism: "Honest criticism is hard to take, particular from a relative, a friend, an acquaintance, or a stranger."

Some of us go so far as to get very defensive about criticism, saying with Benjamin Disraeli, "It is much easier to be critical than correct." Or we side with Kenneth Tynan who said, "A critic is someone who knows the way, but can't drive the car." (Take that, you critics!)

But in our better moments we realize that constructive criticism can be a very worthwhile thing. More than that, it can actually be salvific. Norman Vincent Peale once said, "The trouble with most of us is that we would rather be ruined by praise than saved by criticism." Criticism reminds us that we need feedback from others to help find our way in life.

How would I define criticism? Relying on St. Paul, I'd say criticism is "speaking the truth in love" (Eph 4:15). But when we do offer our criticism, we must humbly remember: we are speaking the truth as we see it. None of us has a monopoly on truth.

Mother Janet Stuart, a nineteenth-century English nun, wrote, "To accept criticism is one of the greatest lessons to be learned in life." I would add, so is learning to give criticism honestly and humbly. This is a grace to pray for: that we may learn to accept and give criticism graciously.

God, teach me to accept and give criticism more graciously.

109) Inviting God to take over

I was telling a friend about a difficult situation I was caught up in. I described the misunderstanding, the confusion, and the pain, hoping to solicit from him a possible solution to my problem or, at least, some well-deserved sympathy.

But, in one way, he gave me neither. And in another way, he gave me both. For when I finished my woeful tale, my friend didn't say, "I'll tell you what to do, Melannie!" Nor "You poor thing! What a terrible mess you're in!" Instead he said, "Well, Melannie, that sounds like a good situation for God to get involved in—and maybe even take over." And he spoke as someone who was speaking from experience.

My friend's response was exactly what I needed to hear. And I realized, the only way God was going to get involved in my messy situation was if I let God get involved. And how was I going to do that? First, by sharing with God everything I had shared with my friend: all the thoughts and feelings, the hurt and anger, the worries and dread—everything. Next, I had to invite God to enter my situation, and I had to ask God to take over.

I had gone to my friend seeking a solution and some sympathy. But he placed before me something far greater: the blazing truth of God's intimate concern for and involvement in my personal life, even during the very messy times.

God, please come into my life today and take over.

110) Working and loafing

The priest asked the kindergartners, "What's your favorite story about Jesus?" One little boy responded instantly: "The story where Jesus loafs and fishes!"

We smile at the little boy's answer, but perhaps he is on to something. When we adults read the gospels, we tend to see a very busy Jesus (much like ourselves). We see a Jesus who is preaching, teaching, traveling, healing, and feeding the multitudes. But do we ever see a loafing Jesus? Are we able to picture him resting against a tree and dangling a fishing line into a river?

Such an image is not too far-fetched really. John's gospel tells us, for example, that Jesus took time to attend a wedding (Jn 2:1–11). And by all accounts, he was leisurely enjoying himself there and had no intention of working that day—that is, not until his mother noticed the wine was running out. The gospels also show us Jesus taking time to dine with friends—Simon the leper (Mk 14:3), Zacchaeus (Lk 19:5–10), and Mary and Martha (Lk 10:38–42). He was so relaxed once that he fell asleep in a boat, perfectly content to entrust the chores of sailing to his friends, until the storm grew too fierce for even their experienced hands (Mt 8:23–27). And how did Jesus ever come up with such great stories (the prodigal son, the good Samaritan) and with such vibrant images (the mustard seed, old and new wineskins, bread rising) unless he made time to stop, listen, observe and "recollect in tranquility" all he was experiencing?

Jesus works, yes. The gospels make that clear. But maybe the little kindergartner is right, too. Maybe Jesus also loafs and fishes.

Jesus, help me to balance all my working with loafing.

∝∝∝

111) Emmanuel

The word Emmanuel is an Advent/Christmas word. It is a word first spoken by the prophet Isaiah to King Ahaz. "Look," he says to the king, "the young woman is with child and shall bear a son, and shall name him Emmanuel" (Is 7:14). It is the same name the angel speaks to a distressed Joseph who has just learned that his fiancee is pregnant—and not by him. "Look," says the angel, "the virgin shall conceive and bear a son, and they shall name him Emmanuel" (Mt 1:23). Then the angel adds, "Which means, 'God is with us.'"

Emmanuel. The word invites reflection. God is with us. *Is* with us. Not just was with us—somewhere back then. Not just will be with us—somewhere in the future. But is with us. Here and now. Do we really believe this? If we do, such a belief will color the way we look at everything—from ants to oceans, from people to planets, from pain to ecstasy. It will make us realize, this world can't be that bad a place after all—not if God is here in it too! My personal life can't be that bad either, that insignificant—not if God is with me!

But I had one scripture professor who gave me an additional insight into the word Emmanuel. He said, "The word Emmanuel means more than 'God is with us,' as beautiful as that is. It means something like, 'God is for us.'"

God is for us. God is "pro me." This means that God is not some passive, disinterested bystander in my life. God is on my side, in my corner, actively pulling for me all the way.

Emmanuel. God is with and for us everyday.

God, Emmanuel, help me to realize you are with and for me today.

⇔ ⇔ ⇔

112) All was not calm, all was not bright

At Christmas time we sing the beautiful hymn "Silent Night." In it we say, "All is calm, all is bright." But if we read the story of the first Christmas, we will conclude, "All was not calm, all was not bright."

All was not calm. When Gabriel first appears to Mary, she is "very much perplexed by his words" (Lk 1:29). When Joseph learns that Mary is pregnant, he too is deeply disturbed (Mt 1:18–20). A terribly inconvenient journey from Nazareth to Bethlehem immediately precedes the birth of Jesus. And shortly after that, Joseph's "dream angel" reappears and warns him to pack up his family and hightail it to Egypt. Where's the calm in all of that?

All was not bright. The Christmas story reminds us that sometimes all is not bright; rather, all is darkness, uncertainty, and confusion. Mary's "yes" at the Annunciation was a "yes" of faith—not certainty. She knew very little, if anything, of what lay ahead for her. As we have seen, Joseph too walked not in clarity but in a cloud, being forced to wait for an angel to direct his next move.

The lessons of the Christmas story are clear. We must never make the mistake of expecting our lives to be calm just because we are trying to be good people. Sometimes God's presence in our lives, like in the lives of Mary and Joseph, will be accompanied by serious disturbances. Similarly, we will not always have a clear vision of tomorrow. We will not always see clearly what to do next.

But Christmas reminds us we walk not always in brightness, but always by faith.

God, when my life is not calm and bright, help me to walk by faith.

✀ ✀ ✀

113) God works through all kinds of people

The story of the first Christmas sets before us a marvelous array of individuals: a teenage mother, a conscientious young carpenter, an egotistical emperor, a bevy of angels, a band of hardworking shepherds, a trio of scholarly star gazers, a wise old holy man, an elderly prophetess, and a megalomanical king. And, lest we forget, a baby!

Another lesson we learn from the story of the first Christmas is this: God works through all kinds of people. All kinds. The young and old, the simple and sophisticated, the rich and the poor, the good and the bad. Incredibly, each of the individuals listed above played a role in salvation history. Some did this knowingly, others without a clue. Some did this through their love and goodness, others through their hatred and evil. The amazing thing is that God can use everyone to effect salvation—even me. The only question is this: what kind of a role will I choose to play?

In Romans we read, "We know that all things work together for good for those who love God" (Rom 8:28). Isn't that some of the best news in the entire Good News?

God, work through me today in some small way!

114) Trying to become a good person

In his book *The Moral Intelligence of Children*, Robert Coles recounts a story of a college sophomore who was working her way through Harvard by cleaning some of the rooms of her fellow students. One day she came crying to Coles, telling him how rude some of the students were to her as she cleaned. One pre-med student, with whom she had taken two courses in moral reasoning, was particularly cruel to her. She cried out, "What's the point of knowing good, if you don't keep trying to become a good person?"

Good question. In his Harvard address on "the American scholar" in 1837, Ralph Waldo Emerson stated, "Character is higher than intellect." Most of us know this. We know that being smart doesn't necessarily make us more virtuous. Being educated doesn't automatically make us a better person.

"What's the point of knowing good if you don't keep trying to become a good person?" No point, really. I think of this every time we bury one of our sisters. Some were highly educated. Others were not. But that's not the point as we lower each casket into the ground. The only point is this: did she keep trying to become a good person?

God, help me to keep trying to become a good person.

∞∞∞

115) Enlarging our borders

In the Hebrew Scriptures, the Israelites are very concerned with borders. In the book of Exodus, for example, God says to Moses, "I will cast out nations before you and enlarge your borders" (Ex 34:24). We can almost hear the people yelling, "Yippee! Less land for our enemies! More land for us!" This preoccupation with territorial borders is found in Deuteronomy too: "When the Lord your

God enlarges your territory as he promised you...." (Dt 12:20). Even the psalms speak of borders: "(God) grants peace within your borders" (Ps 147:14). (As a young nun, I lived in a boarding school with fifty-six teenage boarders, and I often prayed fervently, "God, grant peace within our boarders!")

"I will enlarge your borders," God says. What if we think of "borders" not as geographic demarcations, but rather as limits to our own selves? Our borders: "Here is where I end and you begin. This is the extent of my knowledge. These are the perimeters of my love." If we think of borders in these terms, then God's promise, "I will enlarge your borders," takes on new meaning. It means that God will help us to live beyond where we are now, to extend our knowledge, to deepen our understanding, to widen the sweep of our love.

It is not always easy for us to enlarge our lives. We have this natural tendency to want to live our lives with carefully delineated borders, with clearly established lines. It's safer that way. Neater too. But God is always urging us toward "the more." "Grow...expand...stretch...move beyond," God says to us. And sometimes (sadly) we refuse, saying, "I don't wanna!" But sometimes (happily) we say "yes" to God's invitation—even though we may, in the process, cry, "Ouch!"

God, enlarge my borders!

∾∾∾

116) Fear is a funny thing

As his parents go to turn off the light in his bedroom at night, Dennis the Menace begs them, "Please leave the light on!" They reassure him with, "You don't have to be afraid of the dark." To which Dennis replies, "I'm not afraid of the dark. I'm afraid of what's in the dark!"

Fear is a funny thing. Maybe the adjective "funny" isn't exactly appropriate, for fear is a very serious thing. In fact, fear is the underlying cause of many of our most serious problems. Thomas Merton said, for example, that fear was at the root of all war. The eighteenth-century writer Giambattista Casti would agree, for he wrote, "Short is the road that leads from fear to hate." And author Jim Wallis summed it all up when he said, "Our most deadly enemy is fear."

Yet fear isn't always our deadly enemy. Sometimes it can be our friend. A student of mine admitted to her psychologist one day that she had seriously considered suicide. "But I was too afraid to go through with it," she said, almost apologetically. Her psychologist replied, "Sometimes being afraid is a very good thing."

When, then, is fear our enemy and when is it our friend? It is our enemy if it breeds mistrust, greed, hatred, violence, and the like. But it is our friend if it reminds us of the precariousness of human existence, the fragility of relationships, and the very real limits of time and resources. Fear is good if it leads us to take care of, nourish, use wisely, and appreciate.

John MacMurray said that all religions are ultimately concerned with overcoming fear. But he distinguished between what he called illusory religion and real religion. Illusory religion says, "Fear not; trust in God and God will see that none of the things you fear will happen to you." Real religion, on the contrary, says, "Fear not; the things you fear are quite likely to happen to you, but they are really nothing to be afraid of." In other words, darkness in life is very real. But God is in the darkness with us. Or, as the psalmist says to God, "Darkness is not dark to you; the night is as bright as the day" (Ps 139:12).

Jesus knew this. He experienced it through his passion, death, and resurrection. Little wonder, then, he says to us with such conviction, "Fear not, little flock!" (Lk 12:32).

God, you are with me in my darkness. Let me hear you say to me, "Fear not!"

117) New Year's resolutions

Most of us are good at making New Year's resolutions. "I will lose twenty pounds...I will quit smoking...I will spend more time with my family...I will go to Mass more often...." Making resolutions is easy. It's keeping them that's difficult.

That realization led me to wonder what scripture says about making resolutions. Do any individuals in scripture make resolutions? If so, do they break them or keep them?

Scripture is filled with people making resolutions and then breaking them. Sarah resolves to let Abraham father a child by her slave girl, Hagar, but once little Ishmael is born, Sarah chases both Hagar and the baby away (Gn 16:1–6). At the time of the Exodus, Pharaoh resolves to let the Hebrews go (he had been plagued enough!). But as soon as the people start to pull out en masse, Pharaoh abruptly breaks his resolution and charges after them with his army (Ex 14). In the gospels, Peter vows at the Last Supper never to deny Jesus (Mt 26:35), but he soon takes back his words when challenged by a servant girl around a camp fire (Mt 26:69–75). There are many more examples throughout scripture of people making and breaking their resolutions, which only proves: 1) how hard it is to keep a resolution, and 2) how true to life the Bible is.

But the Bible also sets before us individuals who made resolutions and kept them. God, for example! After destroying the earth with that terrible deluge, God resolves never to do that again. He promises Noah, "I will never again curse the ground because of humankind" (Gn 8:21). That's one resolution God has kept—at least according to the last time I looked out my window. But, more importantly, God's biggest resolve is the covenant God establishes with Israel, a covenant built on God's promise, "I will not forget you" (Is 49:15–16).

The biggest proof that God kept this resolution is, of course, the coming of Jesus. Furthermore, Jesus himself makes and keeps some pretty important resolutions. To those burly fisherman on the shore he says, "Follow me, and I will make you fish for people"

(Mk 1:17). That's one resolution Jesus kept. Later, he shares with his apostles his resolve to go to Jerusalem where he will be tortured and killed. When Peter tries to dissuade him from keeping this resolution, Jesus yells at him, calling him "Satan" and a "stumbling block to me!" (Mt 16:21–23). And finally, Jesus promises his apostles that, after being dead for three days, he will rise again (Lk 9:22). Our entire Christian faith rests on the belief that Jesus kept this resolution.

God, help me to make good resolutions and, with your help, to keep them.

118) What's in a name?

In his book *What's in a Name?: Reflections of an Irrepressible Name Collector*, lexicographer Paul Dickson has gathered together some fascinating lists of names—real names—of people and places all over the globe. Here are some of the names he's collected, mostly from U.S. phone books: Magdalena Babblejack, Oneta Beeny, Urban Bowels, Swanora Crudup, Felty Goosehead, Fanny Longbottom, Reveille Peepless, Joop Spit, Cooper Twaddle, and Tosca Zerk.

Dickson also discovered these doctors' names in medical directories: Dr. Couch (psychiatrist), Dr. Fuzzy (optometrist), Dr. Oops (surgeon), and two dental partners Drs. Diggs and Hurtz. (I once knew a podiatrist named Dr. Tozi. I have a friend who, seeing him for the first time, got a little flustered and addressed him as Dr. Footsie!).

Dickson devotes one chapter to a study of first names given to newborn children. One hundred years ago, the top five most popular girls' names were Mary, Catherine, Margaret, Annie, and Rose. Fifty years ago they were Linda, Mary, Barbara, Patricia, and Susan.

Today they are Ashley, Jessica, Stephanie, Samantha, and Amanda. One hundred years ago, the top boys' names were John, William, Charles, George, and Joseph. Fifty years ago: Robert, John, James, Michael and William. Today they are Michael, Christopher, Kevin, Anthony, and Jonathan.

Dickson's delightful book reminds us: 1) names are important, 2) they can also be fun, and 3) what is considered fashionable, changes quickly!

God, remind me today that you call me by name—whatever my name may be!

119) On being perfect

One of the sayings of Jesus that has caused considerable problems for many of us is this: "Be perfect, therefore, as your heavenly Father is perfect" (Mt 5:48). It's the word "perfect" that is the culprit.

I know some individuals who have agonized over that word, beating their breasts until they were black and blue because they had not yet achieved perfection. "But Jesus told us to be perfect!" cried an elderly sister to me once. She was very frustrated by her faults, especially the chronic ones. "If Jesus told us to be perfect, then it has to be possible, right?"

"Not exactly," I said. To begin with, let's remember that only Matthew uses the word "perfect" here. The Lucan parallel uses the word "merciful" (Lk 6:36). Big difference—at least in our English language. In English, the word perfect means flawless. And no human being can lay claim to being flawless—not even the greatest saints. A friend of mine was having difficulty with another brother in his community, a man known for his piety. Said my friend (half in jest and half seriously), "He may be a saint, but he's a real devil to live with!"

"Be merciful as your heavenly Father is merciful." In one way, this goal is even more challenging than being perfect. Why? Because we can be perfect in total isolation. Theoretically, I can be perfect without ever leaving my room. But we can never be merciful unless we are interacting with other people. After all, I can't show mercy unless I have someone else to show mercy to! And, as Hamlet would say, "There's the rub!"

Another way of looking at this saying of Jesus came to me from a scripture professor. She said, "Think of the word perfect as meaning complete." When we strive for perfection, she explained, what we are really striving for is completion, that is, for wholeness. That interpretation also makes more sense to me.

The question we should ask ourselves, then, is not, "How perfect am I?" But "How merciful am I? How far have I progressed toward wholeness?"

Jesus, make me merciful and whole as your heavenly Father is merciful and whole.

∞∞∞

120) St. Valentine's Day

One of my favorite days of the year is Valentine's Day. It ranks almost as high as Christmas and Thanksgiving as far as I am concerned. Why this great fondness for a day that, some would say, is promoted solely to hawk cards, flowers, and candy? Because, whatever its shortcomings, Valentine's Day does us one great service: it reminds us just how precious love is.

And to think it all started with God! What started with God? No, not Valentine's Day. But love started with God. At least that's what St. John tells us: "We love, because God first loved us" (1 Jn 4:19). That's why whenever I think of Valentine's Day I naturally think of God, the greatest lover of them all. And, like all lovers,

God shows the symptoms of someone in love, namely, blindness and foolishness.

God is blind. How else can we explain the fact that humankind has somehow endured all these centuries despite our pettiness, greed, laziness, dishonesty, wars, violence, cruelty, and all the other evils too numerous and too depressing to list? As one ten-year-old boy said, after becoming more aware of just a few of the injustices in the world, "If I was God, I would've zapped human beings a long time ago!"

But the truth is, God has not zapped us. Obviously, then, God is blind—or at least far more patient than the ten-year-old boy above! Or perhaps it's not that God is blind, but rather God sees things differently than we do. Didn't God say as much through the prophet Isaiah? "My thoughts are not your thoughts, nor are your ways my ways" (Is 55:8). Translation: "My way of seeing and doing things is not your way."

Like any lover, God does foolish things in the name of love. One foolish thing God did was to give us free will, thus opening the door to unspeakable sins of all kinds. Yes, but the gift of free will is precisely the gift that makes all love possible. With infinite wisdom, God must have weighed all things in a balance and opted for love. How crucial love must be!

Which is exactly what Valentine's Day celebrates. It calls us to celebrate the love we experience from family and friends. And it reminds us to give thanks to the source of that love, God, the greatest lover of them all!

God, thank you for the gift of love.

❧❧❧

121) Quotes on God

God has a history of using the insignificant to accomplish the impossible. (Richard Exley)

When God measures a person, God puts the tape around the heart instead of the head. (Anonymous)

God does not always smooth the path, but sometimes God puts springs in the wagon. (Marshall Lucas)

God is the minimum as well as the maximum. (Nicholas of Cusa)

Whatever God does, the first outburst is always compassion. (Meister Eckhart)

God, help me to know and love you more.

122) I yawned at Mass today

...right at the consecration. A big yawn, too. Just as the priest was pronouncing the words, "This is my body.... This is my blood." As soon as I realized what I was doing, I covered my mouth, of course. But it was too late. Others saw me, I'm sure. But even if they didn't, I was aware of what I had done. Priest: "This is my body...." Me: "HO-HUM!"

Afterwards I scolded myself. "How could you yawn during the consecration of the Mass?" I asked. "During one of the most sacred events in the universe?" My answer? A humble, "I don't always measure up to my beliefs."

None of us completely measures up to the things we profess to believe in. We pray, "Thy will be done" and yet we balk every time God's will causes us the least inconvenience. We proclaim "universal charity" and yet we cling to our prejudices or even ignore our elderly parents. We say prayer means a lot to us, but given the choice, we opt for hours in front of the TV.

The cure for this? It starts with humble awareness—awareness of those times when we do fall short of incarnating our religious beliefs. (Strictly speaking, if we think we're hypocrites, we aren't.

Not really. Genuine hypocrites don't even realize they're hypocrites. That's what makes them so hard to help.)

My yawn at Mass wasn't the first yawn nor will it be the last. And, seen in perspective, a yawn is small and insignificant compared to some of the other ways we may fall short in our faith. But today my yawn did me a great service, by leading me to see there's often a gap between what I believe and what I do—a gap bridged only by God's mercy.

God, help me to incarnate my religious beliefs better, and show me mercy when I don't.

123) Homilies

A preacher began his sermon to his new congregation with these words: "As I see it, my job is to talk to you; your job is to listen. If you finish before I do, just raise your hand."

Seriously, the sermon or homily is one of the most important parts of the Mass. For that's the part where the homilist takes the readings of the day and applies them to the here and now, to this specific congregation. And that's vital. Otherwise, we may be tempted to think of the readings as a message for an earlier age or for "those other people over there." Because the scripture readings are so old, we can sometimes think of them as merely a family heirloom—our great-great-grandmother's china tea cup, for example—something we cherish and admire, yes, but something we would never think of actually using.

But a good homily won't allow us to do that. A good homily won't let us get away with saying things like this: "How dense those apostles were!" "Look at how blind those Pharisees are!" "Why don't those Corinthians pay more attention to St. Paul's words, anyway?" No, a good homily will make us say things like this: "Sometimes we're as dense as those apostles." "What are we blind to in our own lives?" "How can we put into practice what St. Paul is telling us today?"

God, continue to speak to me through scripture and homilies.

124) The school crossing guard

I was driving by the Catholic church at about 2:30 in the afternoon. It was the week before Christmas and it was pouring rain. As I waited for the light to change, I spotted her: the school crossing guard. She was wearing big boots, jeans, a bright orange vest, and a yellow rain cap. And she was holding in her hand a big red STOP sign. But here's the fun part! She was standing inside the life-size Christmas crèche in front of the church! Yes, there she was, standing next to St. Joseph—who didn't seem at all surprised to see her there either! Apparently, while waiting for the dismissal bell to ring, the woman had used her common sense and had taken refuge from the rain in the manger.

Seeing her there, I laughed out loud. What a source for meditation! First, it was as if she was telling all passersby to STOP! STOP your racing around for a minute, STOP your frenzied Christmas shopping, STOP your worrying, STOP your complaining about the weather, and remember the real reason for this season: the birth of this little baby boy.

In addition, she was, by her placement, physically demonstrating what many spiritual writers (most notably St. Ignatius of Loyola) encouraged us to do: to place ourselves into the scripture stories, that is, to immerse ourselves in the heart of the action. Here she was, literally putting her whole self directly into that manger! St. Ignatius would have been proud!

And finally, the woman looked perfectly at ease in that manger—as if she belonged there. She looked comfortable and safe, too. But she wouldn't remain in that shelter for very long. For in a few minutes the dismissal bell would ring, the children would come pouring out of the school, and she would begin her work, her ministry, if you will: helping the children to cross the street in safety. At Christmas, God calls us into the manger to adore. But then God sends us forth into the world, where, like this school crossing guard, we help to lead others safely home.

Jesus, help me to immerse myself in scripture.

∞∞∞

125) Will the magic happen again today?

Sister Laura Wingert, SND, is an artist and a good friend of mine. A teacher of art for over twenty-five years, she has won many awards and prizes for her various works—drawings, paintings, sculpture, photography, weavings, and (her specialty) clay pots.

Laura and I have had numerous conversations about the creative process. We both speak of the "terror" that precedes our creating something—she, the terror of the empty canvas or unformed lump of clay, I, the terror of the empty page or blank computer screen. What we are both admitting to is this: the ability to create something—anything—is mostly gift. Realizing this, Laura (every time she sits down to draw) and I (every time I sit down to write) wonder: "Will I be inspired today? Will the magic happen again?"

The magic, of course, is the ability to fashion something that transcends our personal limitations, something that surprises and delights us, the creator, as much as it may surprise and delight our audience or readers. Sure, the magic may have happened yesterday and the day before—and perhaps even a thousand times before. But the question always remains: will the magic happen today?

This doesn't mean that artists don't work hard. We do. Very hard. But deep in our hearts we know that inspiration is something we have little, if any, control over. We all rely on something (someone?) beyond ourselves to produce what we do. The ancient Greeks had a name for this thing: the muse, they called it. Laura and I prefer to call it "the creative and holy Spirit."

Being artists is good for the soul. If nothing else, it keeps us humble.

Holy Spirit, make the magic happen in my life today.

126) Impure thoughts

When I was a young girl, I was bothered by impure thoughts. Don't get me wrong. I still have so-called impure thoughts; it's just that now I'm not as bothered by them as I once was. Let me explain.

First, a story. There were two elderly brothers: Bob, 94, and Joe, 92. One day someone asked Joe, "At what age do you stop having impure thoughts?" Joe grinned and said sheepishly, "You'd better ask Bob. He's older."

The story implies that, as long as we are alive and well, we will probably be plagued by good, wholesome impure thoughts every now and then. (I'm sure, for example, that I'm not the only person who even gets them during Mass!) I use those words "good" and "wholesome" here with good reason, for many so-called impure thoughts are really only natural, spontaneous, biologically induced responses. They signal to us, "Guess what? You're still very much alive!" Impure thoughts, as we were taught years ago, are problematic when they 1) are chronic, 2) lead us to bring harm to others, and 3) interfere with normal, happy, healthy, altruistic living.

Another story: A young boy went to confession and confessed that he had had impure thoughts. "Did you entertain them?" the priest asked him. "No," the boy replied. "They entertained me!"

We must put things like impure thoughts into perspective with other issues in our lives. It is amazing, for example, that of all the topics Jesus addressed he mentioned sexual sins only a couple of times. He devoted far more time and attention to other more important issues like love, forgiveness, and concern for the poor.

Another story, this time a true one, summarizes what I am saying here. An auxiliary bishop in Brazil was asked to comment on the phenomenon of toplessness on the beaches of his diocese. The bishop replied, "I am more worried about the nudity of those who have no clothes to wear."

God, thank you for the gift of sexuality. May my struggles with this gift never distract me from more important concerns in my life—like loving the poor.

127) Emperor penguins

Recently I read an article on Emperor penguins by Glenn Oeland in *National Geographic* magazine. Of all penguins, Emperors are the only ones that stay in Antarctica even during the winter. Amazingly, some 400,000 of them actually breed in winter—in temperatures of forty degrees below zero! Says Oeland, "The simple fact that they succeed (in breeding) is a source of wonderment."

After the usual two-week courtship, the female lays a single egg the size of a softball. Then she goes on a two-month feeding spree, leaving her husband at home to incubate the egg, "with only his body fat to sustain him." The male keeps the egg on top of his feet for sixty-five days. He does nothing else during this time but stand and incubate. Little wonder he loses up to one-half of his body fat in the process. When the chick finally hatches, it spends the first two months in either of its parents' brood pouch. If the chick should tumble from that haven, it can freeze to death in less than two minutes.

As naturalist Graham Robertson puts it, "Emperors live on the cutting edge of life itself." They manage to survive for chiefly two reasons. First, they possess an extremely dense plumage—eighty feathers per square inch. Secondly, during blizzards, they forget all about their individual territories and coalesce into a single mass. Says Robertson, "Like people in a crisis, they forget their differences and rally together."

And so again, another member of the animal kingdom can inspire us human beings. "Wear thick feathers," these penguins tell us (or thick skin, if you prefer). "And during the blizzards of life, forget about retaining your territory and rally together."

God, give me thick plumage to withstand life's bitter winds.
And let me not wait for a crisis to rally together with others.

❧❧❧

128) My mother and
the vacuum cleaner bags

One day my mother went into a vacuum cleaner store to buy some bags for her sweeper. She gave the man the serial number of the bags she needed. He went into the back and soon came out with a package of bags. My mother checked the number on it and said, "But this isn't the number I gave you." The man replied, "I know, but trust me, these will fit."

My mother charged the bags and left. When she got home, however, and tried to put one of the new bags into her sweeper, it didn't fit. Perturbed, she returned to the store a few days later and asked for a refund. The man pointed to a small sign in the window that said, "No cash refunds." My mother calmly walked out of the store, taking the useless bags with her.

She could have let the whole thing end there. She had been

taken, she knew. But, after all, it was for only $16.00. Why fight it? But in telling me the story, my mother said, "It wasn't the money. It was the fact that if this man cheated me and got away with it, then he'd be more likely to cheat the next little old lady that came in."

To try to prevent that, my mother took action. To make it short, she reported the incident to the Better Business Bureau, the local TV station, and her credit card company. The Bureau and TV station put some pressure on the man, but because of the sign in his window, they couldn't do too much. But when my mother told her story to the credit card company, they blocked payment on the bags. Within a few days, the man called my mother, telling her to bring back the bags and he'd give her a full refund. Said my mother, "You mail me my refund first, and then I'll mail you the bags." He did. She did.

This story is more than a tale about a determined woman who got some justice. It is a story about a woman who knows that everything that happens to her can and often does have an impact on other people. My mother was acting not only for herself and "other little old ladies," as she remarked. She was acting for all of us working toward a more just world.

God, make me appreciate that everything that happens to me can and often does affect others. And help me to work toward a more just world.

∞ ∞ ∞

129) Remember to remember

One of the most frequently used words in scripture is the word remember. In the Hebrew Scriptures, we are told over and over again that God is someone who remembers: "And God remembered Noah (Gn 8:1)....God remembered Abraham (Gn

19:29)....God remembered Rachel (Gn 30:22)....God remembered his covenant" (Ex 2:24).

Over and over again in scripture God reminds people to remember: "Remember the Sabbath day (Ex 20:8)....Remember my covenant with Jacob (Lv 26:42)....Remember all the commandments" (Nm 15:39). The psalms, too, are often prayers asking God to remember: "Be mindful of your mercy" (Ps 25:6); or to forget: "Do not remember the sins of my youth" (Ps 25:7).

The New Testament also shows how important remembering is. Only one-tenth of the lepers remembered to come back and thank Jesus for being cured. Jesus obviously appreciates the fact that at least one of them remembered to say "thanks" (Lk 17:11–19). Several times Jesus warns his apostles of his passion and death, "so that when their hour comes you may remember that I told you about them" (Jn 16:4). And as Jesus was hanging on the cross, one of the men being executed with him begs, "Jesus, remember me when you come into your kingdom." And Jesus replies, "Truly I tell you, today you will be with me in Paradise" (Lk 23:42–43). In other words, "Don't worry. I'll remember you!"

When I give talks and retreats, I usually begin by telling the people that much of what I am going to say, they already know. My job as speaker or retreat director is largely to remind them of things already nestling in their minds and hearts. As a writer, I'm doing much the same thing. Probably as you're reading this book, you find yourself saying, "I know that already, but it's good to remember."

Jesus, remember me! And teach me to remember to remember!

✑✑✑

130) The good thing about being an addict

I have several friends who are in A.A. One said to me the other day, "The good thing about being an addict is you know you can never get well without help."

His words surprised me. I had never imagined there was anything good about being an addict, whether you had surrendered yourself to something obviously destructive (like drugs or alcohol) or to something less noticeably lethal (like chocolate, computer games, romance novels) or to something apparently noble (like church ministry!).

In his book *Intimacy with God*, Thomas Keating, a Cistercian monk, makes the claim that we all suffer from some form of addiction. In other words, we all have areas in our lives where we regularly surrender ourselves to what he calls "the consequences of original sin," namely, illusion, concupisence, and weakness of will. According to Keating, we must admit our powerlessness to God before we can begin to turn our lives around. Members of A.A. know this. They've done it. It only makes sense, doesn't it? If we're drowning and we can't swim, it's only natural to yell "HELP!" and allow someone else to throw us a line.

In his second letter to the Corinthians, St. Paul tells of being given "a thorn...a messenger of Satan to torment me" (2 Cor 12: 7). No one knows for sure what that thorn was. But it is not too far-fetched to think of it in terms of some form of addiction. Whatever it was, Paul begs God three times to take this torment away. But God replies: "My grace is sufficient for you, for power is made perfect in weakness" (2 Cor 12:9).

God, may I acknowledge my addictions, my weaknesses, and yell for help.

∞ ∞ ∞

131) For a God I know and love

I awoke one morning with this startling realization: "I'm working my tail off for a God I barely know." For there I was, a full-time high school teacher (teaching six classes) with a host of extracurricular activities on the side (like drama, the senior class, and the school newspaper, among others). In addition I had community and family commitments to attend to, plus the ever-nagging sense that I wanted to (and should!) be writing for publication. And underlying all of this was the fact that I was a Sister, someone who professed to be serious about developing a strong, personal relationship with God through prayer. (Here I was a "Bride of Christ," and I felt I hadn't even shaken hands with my Bridegroom yet!)

To put it mildly, I was exhausted. And frustrated. I found myself asking, "Is this the way life is supposed to be lived? Is this what God really wants for me?" Eventually, with the help of friends and some good spiritual direction, I answered both of those questions with a firm "No." Through the course of time, I began modifying my life by modifying my choices.

First, I had to face honestly that having such a heavy workload was partly my own doing. My desire to please others played a key role in my taking upon myself more and more responsibilities. My wanting to do everything perfectly (which often meant doing everything myself) was also a contributing factor. Plus, possessing considerable talents and thinking I could do it all, I had a hard time asking others for help. In addition, I actually feared not being busy, for my work helped distract me from aspects of my self and my life that I preferred not to face. Undergirding all of these factors was a warped image I had of God as one who prized duty and personal responsibility more than anything else—more than common sense, trust, humility, fun, and even love.

Love. It always came back to this for me. I pictured myself suddenly dying in the midst of all this frenzied activity, and asked myself, What would people say about me given these two choices: "Boy, she worked hard!" or "Boy, she loved much!"? I knew in my heart which one I wanted it to be. And I also knew where I had to start to make it so: with loving God. Which meant, spending quality time with God in prayer.

Work and love are not mutually exclusive, by any means. In fact, it is often through our work that we express our love. But the truth remains: work and love are not synonymous. If we're working our tail off, we should pause long enough to ask ourselves honestly: are we doing it mostly for ourselves, or are we doing it for the God we know and love?

My God, may I know and love you better!

132) Looking for God in unfamiliar places

W. Paul Jones is a professor of ecumenism at a Methodist seminary. A social activist and a family brother of the Trappist order, Jones offers a fascinating suggestion for furthering ecumenism. What he says, I think, has implications that reach far beyond ecumenism.

Jones suggests that each of us expose ourselves to contrasting expressions of church. He suggests, for example, that a Quaker enter a cathedral for Christmas midnight Mass, that a Southern Baptist spend time in a Benedictine monastery, that a Trappist monk participate in an inner-city storefront church speaking in tongues, and that a TV evangelist spend a few hours with a hermit whose motto over the door is that of St. Bernard of Clairvaux: "Love to be unknown." And finally, that a bishop share communion with a handleless cup in an Appalachian shack.

Jones' suggestion is marvelous! If followed in all areas of our life, it would make us break out of our own "comfort zone" and explore foreign lands or even "other planets." Doing such a thing could broaden our perspective, deepen our spirituality, and enrich our entire lives. It could lead us to find God in places we haven't looked yet. With this in mind, we might want to do something like this:

Befriend someone very different from ourselves…attend a service in a church very unlike our own…read a book or see a movie we ordinarily wouldn't read or see…listen to a radio station we've never listened to before…pray in a place we've never prayed before.

God, help me to look for you in unfamiliar places.

133) Crossword puzzles

Quick! What's a five-letter word for "gambler"? "Player"? No, that's six letters. "Bettor"? No, that's six, too. Here's a hint: it begins with the letter "D." Give up? It's "dicer"! Okay, here's another one. Give me a five-letter word for the verb "propose." "Urge"? No, that's four letters. I'll give you a hint. It begins with "O." That's right, "offer"!

In case you haven't guessed it, I like crossword puzzles. I love the challenge of finding the answers, those exact words the puzzle is looking for. In each instance, only one word is correct, too. Both "raze" and "ruin" might fit in the squares as synonyms for "devastate," but only one is the right answer—its rightness being determined by whether it fits with the other answers around it.

I used to devise crossword puzzles for my students as a fun way to review key terms before a test. I'd hand out my homemade puzzles, and the students would work alone or in groups to complete them. The first finished won. I was amazed at how excited even sophisticated high schoolers got when, after struggling over a clue for a long time, they finally came up with the correct answer. When they did, they often let out an audible sigh that was a mixture of delight and relief. Then they'd give me a knowing glance that said, "I got it!"

Life is sometimes like a crossword puzzle. We agonize over the clues it gives us. We often propose a variety of answers as to its meaning. But then comes the day we finally come up with the correct answer. Maybe it's "love" or "faith" or "hope" or "forgiveness." And when we do get the answer, we let out an audible sigh that is a mixture of delight and relief. And we whisper to God, "I got it!"

Quoting Isaiah, John the Baptist announced the coming of God's kingdom with these words: "Every valley shall be filled, and every mountain and hill shall be made low, and the crooked shall be made straight, and the rough ways be made smooth" (Lk 3:5). He could just as easily have added, "And every word will come into the crossword puzzle!"

God, help me to get it.

❧❧❧

It may be that God has the eternal
appetite for infancy.

—*G. K. Chesterton*

SPRING

134) The newborn calf

I spot the newborn calf out in the pasture today trying out his new legs. Everything about him is new: not only his legs, but also his eyes, ears, nose, mouth, tail, and spotless white coat. Everything! Brand new! Born just a few days ago, he's jumping up and down all over the place this afternoon. As he romps around the pasture, I can almost hear him calling to his mother nearby, "Hey, Ma! Lookee at what I can do with these legs!" And he kicks his little rear end up in the air a few times in an effort to impress her.

His mother, however, is not impressed. In fact, she isn't even paying any attention to him, for, as soon as she spotted me coming, she stopped what she was doing. Standing motionless now, she eyes me with fear and suspicion. I can almost hear her warning me, "Stay away! Don't you dare come any closer!" The immobile cow is a sharp contrast to the frisky little calf who hasn't even noticed my approach yet, so taken up is he with the fascination of his legs!

As I watch the two of them, I find myself identifying almost exclusively with the cow. I, too, have been motionless these past several weeks—maybe "stuck" is a better word. I, too, have been eyeing with suspicion everything and everyone that comes near me. I too, have been silently warning others, "Stay away! Don't come any closer!" As a result, I feel stodgy—much like that mother cow. I feel old too—or at least too used to things. The more I watch mother and son, the more I find myself envying the joy and exuberance of this newborn calf, and pitying the jadedness and staidness of his mother.

As we graze in the pasture of life, I don't think God intends for us to turn into fixed, timorous, "been-there, done-that" old cows. I think God wants us to retain some of the playful exuberance of a newborn calf—no matter how old we get, how many responsibilities we bear, how many dangers we encounter. We will succeed in doing this, too, only if we remember these things: Never take the incredible gift of life for granted. Never get too used to things—to anything. Never forget that everything we have—legs, other cows, the pasture itself—is a blessing. And never forget to entrust our safekeeping into the hands of God, our loving Creator.

God, help me never to get too used to your blessings.

ꝗ ꝗ ꝗ

135) Conversion

In the Acts of the Apostles we read of the conversion of St. Paul (Acts 9:1–19). Saul (later called Paul) is on his way to Damascus to round up some Christians to drag back to Jerusalem as fresh meat for the lions. Suddenly "a light from heaven" flashes around Saul, hurling him to the ground. Temporarily blinded, he hears the voice of Jesus asking him, "Saul, Saul, why do you persecute me?" We know how the story ends. Saul makes a 180-degree turn in his life. Embracing the Christian faith with a passion, Paul eventually becomes the leading evangelizer in the early church.

On the surface, it looks as if Paul's conversion was not only radical, but instantaneous. One day seething persecutor, next day ardent devotee. But if we read an earlier story, namely the stoning of St. Stephen, we find this intriguing sentence: "Then they dragged (Stephen) out of the city and began to stone him; and the witnesses laid their cloaks at the feet of a young man named Saul" (Acts 7:58). Who can measure the impact Stephen's courageous martyrdom had on the impressionable young Saul (an impact, perhaps, that even Saul was not aware of at the time)? Saul's conversion process could have actually begun with Stephen's stoning—or even earlier. And only later, on the road to Damascus, did that process come to fruition.

I, for one, have always been a little suspicious of "instant conversions." I don't deny they can happen; I just think gradual conversions are not only more trustworthy, they are also the norm.

In *Surprised by Joy*, C.S. Lewis describes his own conversion, a rather lengthy and convoluted one. In vivid and even humorous terms, he describes the culminating moment of that conversion, when, alone in his room, he finally knelt down and admitted that "God was God." Contrasting himself with the prodigal son, he writes: "The Prodigal Son at least walked home on his own feet. But who can duly adore that Love which will open the high gates to a prodigal who is brought in kicking, struggling, resentful and darting his eyes in every direction for a chance to escape?" Lewis dubbed himself fittingly "the most...reluctant convert in all England."

God, continue to convert me to walk in your ways—no matter how long it takes.

❧ ❧ ❧

136) Offer it up

As children, when our TV went on the blink and we'd complain because we couldn't watch our favorite shows, my parents would say, "Offer it up." In school, when we couldn't go outside for recess because of the rain, the teachers would say, "Offer it up." And when we didn't eat any candy during Lent, we knew why we were doing it: we were offering it up.

Offer it up, "it" being this disappointment, this pain, this sacrifice. "Offer up" meaning (presumably) to God.

Since Vatican II, the phrase "offer it up" has fallen into disfavor. One reason could be because, in the past, the phrase had been so abused. Sometimes "Offer it up!" was merely a euphemism for, "Shut up!": "The Mass is meaningless to me." "Offer it up!" "My husband drinks." "Offer it up!" "You mean I can't be an altar boy just because I'm a girl?" "Offer it up!"

Too bad the phrase has become unpopular, for it continues to express a dynamic that is still very integral to our Christian faith. "Offer it up" does not mean we should shut up and suffer, or that we cannot and should not make changes. It does mean, however, that some things are within our control, and some things are beyond our control. And like the so-called "serenity prayer" says, we should pray for the wisdom to know the difference.

Furthermore, "Offer it up" reminds us that we are not in this thing (life!) alone. We are in it together, with God (first and foremost) and with a whole host of others—the people next door as well as the people on the other side of the world, those individuals who are already deceased and those who haven't even been born yet. We offer things up for others—that is, we make sacrifices for them—precisely because that's what Jesus did. Jesus laid down his life for us. Translation? He offered it up for us.

Jesus, help me to offer up my life for others, as you did.

ꝗ꙼ ꝗ꙼ ꝗ꙼

137) Wonder: behold!

Wonder is a holy and forceful thing. According to journalist Bill Moyers, wonder has the power to make people moral. In his book *A World of Ideas II*, Moyers describes watching the launch of Apollo 17 in 1975. He describes the rocket rising off the launching pad amid brilliant flames and deafening thunder. He tells how a sense of wonder fills everyone as they watch the mighty ship go up and up and up. They gaze in amazement as the first stage ignites a beautiful blue flame. Writes Moyer, the rocket "becomes like a star, but you realize there are humans on it." As the ship soars out of sight, a hush falls over the crowd.

Later, as the people begin to leave, Moyer describes the effect that the launch has had on them: "People just get up quietly, helping each other up. They're kind. They open doors. They look at one another, speaking quietly and interestedly. These were suddenly moral people because the sense of wonder, the experience of wonder, had made them moral."

Perhaps that's why Jesus encouraged us so many times to "behold" things. Behold the lilies of the field...behold the birds of the air...behold the bread rising...behold the wine fermenting. Maybe Jesus, too, believed morality begins with wonder.

Jesus, teach me to "behold" things so I may be made more moral.

⚘ ⚘ ⚘

138) Quotes on life

In making a living today, many people no longer leave any room for life. (Joseph Sizoo)

One never finds life worth living. One always has to make it worth living. (Harry Emerson Fosdick)

We only live once, but if we do it right, once is enough. (Anonymous)

Let us so live that when we come to die, even the undertaker will be sorry. (Mark Twain)

Life is not a problem to be solved, a question to be answered. Life is a mystery to be contemplated, wondered at, savored. (Anthony DeMello, SJ)

God, help me savor life.

⚘ ⚘ ⚘

139) "It's all right"

In her book *The Summer of the Great Grandmother*, Madeleine L'Engle describes in poignant detail how she cared for her elderly mother during her final months. Mentally confused and physically incapacitated, her mother is periodically overcome with fear. One time in particular, the old woman, now confined to her bed, reaches for her daughter and cries, "I'm scared, I'm scared." L'Engle describes what she does:

"I put my arms around her and hold her. I hold her as I held my children when they were small and afraid of the night....I hold her as she, once upon a time and long ago, held me. And I say the same words, the classic, maternal, instinctive words of reassurance: 'Don't be afraid. I'm here. It's all right.'"

L'Engle goes on to say that, even though she does not understand those words, "I mean them." What's more, she says those words of reassurance are behind everything she does—from writing books to cooking meals, from talking to her children to walking the dog. "Don't be afraid. I'm here. It's all right."

L'Engle's words echo the reassuring words Jesus says over and over again in the gospels—when he raises Jairus' daughter (Lk 8:40–56), when he comes to the apostles across the water (Mt 14:22–27), when he speaks of his impending passion and death (Jn 16:22), and when he appears to his apostles after the resurrection (Jn 20:19–29). "Don't be afraid. I'm here. It's all right."

Most of us are realistic enough to know that we do, indeed, have much to be afraid of in life. We also know how little we can do to insure the safety of those we love. But coupled with this stark realism is our consoling Christian faith—a faith which reassures us, "Don't be afraid...Jesus is here...It's all right."

Jesus, help me to speak words of reassurance to someone today.

🧩 🧩 🧩

140) Naming things

In early March I spot two crocuses out by the side of the house. One is light purple; the other, bright yellow. I greet them cheerfully, "Hi, little fellas! How are you?" And I stoop down to pet them, spontaneously dubbing the purple one Charlie and the yellow one April. The next morning when I wake up and look out the window, I see, to my surprise, a heavy blanket of snow. "How pretty!" I say without thinking. Then suddenly, remembering the crocuses (*my* crocuses), I gasp, "Oh, no!" instantly fearing the worst. For some inexplicable reason, I now feel concern for those two crocuses, as if my noticing them and naming them has somehow made me partially responsible for their well-being.

Then it hits me: so that's why God made Adam name all the animals in the Garden of Eden (Gn 2:20)! So that Adam would first notice them and then, by naming them, realize he was partially responsible for their well-being. In short, so Adam would care for them.

All caring begins with noticing and naming.

God, help me to notice and name things today so I might care for them.

✾ ✾ ✾

141) Throwing seed with open hands

In one of his talks, Paul Molinari, SJ, said: "You must not be concerned about the fruit of what you do. You must be generous in throwing the seed with open hands, without becoming discouraged when the fertile soil seems scarce."

Spring is the season of the year that reminds us of this great truth. We need not worry about the fruit of what we do. We need only be generous with our sowing. This is no small task for us.

Understandably, we'd all like to see the fruit of our labors, or, at least a few green shoots sprouting from the seed we've sown so painstakingly. For when we see no fruit, what happens? We are tempted (quite naturally) to hold back some of our seed. "I must save some for the next season," we explain. Or we ask, "Why waste my seed here?"

God, on the other hand, would have us sow generously, extravagantly, even wastefully—wherever we may find ourselves. We can afford to, too, knowing full well that we are not the lord of the harvest. God is. We are mere sowers. As such, we need concern ourselves solely with this: how wide is the arc of our throw, how open our hands.

Lord of the Harvest, teach me to throw my seed with open hands.

❧ ❧ ❧

142) A parent's love

A few years back, I was at a mall with a nun friend of mine. It was early spring, but cold and windy. While there, we, by chance, ran into my friend's mother. After the usual exchange of warm greetings, her mother suddenly became serious. Tugging the sleeve of her daughter's jacket, she asked sternly, "Is that jacket warm enough?"

I had to smile. My friend was no little child. She was in her early thirties and had left home years ago. But here was her mother, still worrying whether her jacket was warm enough for her. It reminded me of my own mother. When I was about eleven years old, I had a foot problem that necessitated regular trips to a foot doctor until I was seventeen. Today, many years later, my mother still occasionally asks me, "How are your feet, Honey?"

These mothers' questions made me wonder: do mothers ever stop worrying about their kids? Do parents ever stop being parents? Someone once said that when two people have a baby, they make a commitment for the next eighteen years. But I think they make a commitment for life. Once a parent, always a parent, it seems to me. There's no retirement from parenthood. Even after their children are out of the nest and may even have nests of their own, parents still worry about their children. And when parents become grandparents, they start worrying about their grandchildren, too. And then their great-grandchildren!

A parent's love is a lot like God's love. For God's love, too, goes on and on, from generation to generation. God can't retire from being God either. As the psalmist says, "God's steadfast love endures forever, and God's faithfulness to all generations" (Ps 100:5).

God, help me to reflect your everlasting love.

❧ ❧ ❧

143) "Like *what?*"

One of the Jesuit novices was telling about his first day at his new ministry assignment, a detention home for girls—all of whom were the proverbial "streetwise." He was introduced to a group of them with the words, "And Dan is a biochemist."

Immediately one of the girls picked up on that. "Boy, I bet *you* make a lot of money!"

Dan replied, "No, not really."

Not in the least bit shy, she asked, "Why not?"

"You see," Dan said, "I'm studying to be a priest."

"A *priest*?!" she gasped in disbelief. (Dan is a nice-looking twenty-six-year-old!) "What are you doing a thing like that for? You don't *have* to be a priest, ya know. You can go to church on Sunday, be a biochemist, *and* make lots of money."

"I know," said Dan. "It's just that I think there are more important things in life than making a lot of money."

To which the girl asked in sincerity and shock, "Like *what?*"

I don't know how Dan answered that question. With a single word perhaps—like love? All I know is, I sat with that question for quite a while tonight, trying to answer it for myself. "So, you believe there are more important things in life than making a lot of money, right? Like *what?*"

God, reveal to me all those things in life that are more important than money.

✦ ✦ ✦

144) On aging

A friend of mine was beginning to feel a little arthritis in her joints. She said to me, "The other day I woke up and wondered, 'When did I get my mother's body?'"

I know what she means. I crawled out of bed one morning and I noticed a kink in my lower back. A week or so later, my right wrist began to hurt. And lately, I've been getting these sinus headaches. To all of these things I register my protest to the cosmos: "But my back and wrist never used to hurt! And I never used to get sinus headaches!" To which the cosmos replies, "Welcome to mid-life-hood!"

How do we react to the natural aging process? Do we fret? Do we deny it? Are we afraid? All of these responses are perfectly natural. Getting older is no picnic—unless you're still under twenty-one. And our society offers us little help for facing the aging process except beauty creams, hair coloring, and vitamin supplements.

For many, even death itself isn't as foreboding as is aging. Someone once remarked, "It's not death that I worry about. It's the process of getting old." She was voicing what many of us fear most: that gradual process of losing things, from our hearing to our friends; and of losing control over our finances, our bodies, our minds.

Rich Heffern, assistant editor of *Praying* magazine, writes, "Acceptance of aging, to me, seems like an acid test for our spirituality. Do we trust that the cosmos we come from is ultimately benign, that God is really love?" Good question. In the end, it's the only question.

Thank God we have individuals in our midst who are aging well—parents, aunts and uncles, elderly members of our communities. These are individuals who, despite their increasing infirmity, continue to smile and laugh, to find enchantment in life, and to come up with creative ways to serve others!

God, as I continue to age, may I continue to trust that the cosmos is benign and you are really love.

⚘ ⚘ ⚘

145) The parable of the brownies

When I was a little girl, I liked to bake things from scratch, especially cakes and cookies. One day, early in my baking career, I said enthusiastically to my brother Paul, "Today I'm going to bake you some brownies." My brother smiled, obviously pleased with my announcement. While he went for a walk in the woods, I set about my task.

I did everything the recipe told me to do. I creamed the eggs and sugar, sifted the flour, melted the unsweetened chocolate, and mixed the batter. Finally, I proudly put the pan of brownies into the oven to bake. Several minutes later, as I was cleaning up the dishes, I was shocked by what I saw sitting on the counter: the bowl of sifted flour! I had forgotten to put in the flour! In my naiveté, I said to myself, "Oh well, it probably won't make much of a difference," and I poured the unused flour back into the bag.

Needless to say, the absence of flour did make a difference. A big difference! When I took the pan out of the oven, there were my brownies: approximately one-fourth of an inch high, a thin layer of chocolate goo on the bottom of the pan. To this day, my brothers still tease me about the time I made brownies without flour. (In my defense, however, I just want to say that they still ate them!)

What does this story have to do with Christian living? To me, it's something of a parable. In his first letter to the Corinthians, St. Paul gave us the recipe for happy living, namely, faith, hope, and love. Then he added, "And the greatest of these is love" (1 Cor 13:13). Perhaps we could also say, "And the flour in the recipe is love."

Jesus, help me to put all your ingredients into my life— especially love.

✤ ✤ ✤

146) Silence

We live in a noisy world. Cars speed down our streets, planes soar over our heads, the baby cries next door, the TV blares in the living room, and the telephone rings all hours of the day and night. (As I typed that last sentence, my telephone rang!) Coupled with these obvious noises are other less noticeable ones: the steady humming of our refrigerators, furnaces, air conditioners, computers, and even florescent lights.

In addition to these kinds of noises, we have words. Now, don't get me wrong: I, for one, love words. After all, I make part of my living off words! Yet even I am sometimes overwhelmed by all the words that bombard me in a single day, plus all the words I am compelled or choose to generate each day. When I was teaching full-time, for example, I would be totally exhausted at the end of a school day. When I tried to figure out the source of my fatigue, I came up with one of the leading culprits: words! I realized that on any given day I was forced to answer literally hundreds of questions from my students—questions like, What page are we on? What's our homework again? How come we've got to learn this stuff? Did you correct our tests yet? How am I doing in your class? Did you find my notebook? What are we going to do in class today? How come you didn't give me an A?

The Trappist monks have a saying: "Speak only when it improves the silence." If only the rest of the world would live by that maxim! But the reality is, for most of us, noise and words are the norm; silence, the exception.

But just because silence is the exception, doesn't mean we shouldn't make efforts to cultivate it in our lives. For throughout the centuries, virtually all spiritual writers have spoken of the necessity of silence in developing a deeper relationship with God. Said one, "Only a person who can hear silence will hear the voice of God."

Although it's true God can and does sometimes speak to us through noise, it seems that God's preferred modus operandi is still silence. With this in mind, we might ask ourselves: how do we cultivate silence in our own personal lives?

God, help me to cultivate silence that I may hear your voice.

✴ ✴ ✴

147) Good prayer

In his book *The God Who Fell From Heaven*, Father John Shea tells the story of a woman who one day found a "sock of pot" in her fourteen-year-old son's sock drawer. Angrily, she stomped into the den where her son was watching TV and began to hit him. Later, on her way to church, she met Father Shea and told him what had happened. "I can't stand to look at him," she said.

The woman then went into church and sat in a back pew for quite some time. When she emerged, Shea asked her, "How's it going?"

"I prayed about it," she said.

Shea asked, "What did you find out?"

The woman replied, "He's not all bad and I'm not all good."

Good prayer will do that. It will help us to see things as they really are. It will invite us to compassion. It will keep us humble.

God, may my prayer help me to see things as they really are, invite me to compassion, and keep me humble.

✦ ✦ ✦

148) My football career

Many people are surprised when I tell them that I played football in my youth. What I don't tell them is that I played only one game. More accurately, only one quarter. Okay, okay: I played only a couple of plays! It all happened when I was about thirteen. My two older brothers, along with some other boys in the neighborhood, decided to play football in our front yard. Thinking it would be fun (especially being the only girl), I asked if I could play, too. They said "Yes," although my brother John warned me, "It can get a little rough."

The first few plays were no problem. That's because the other team had the ball, and they scored quickly—on only two plays. Now it was our turn. We got the ball. More specifically, I got the ball. Our quarterback handed it off to me. Cradling it in both arms,

I lowered my head and ran like crazy. What I didn't do was look where I was going. And (as John Madden would say) *boom!* I ran right into my brother John. Although only sixteen, John was already well on his way to becoming over six feet tall. The impact stunned me—and John hadn't even tackled me! He had just stood there! I dropped the ball, went down in a heap, and instantly lost all interest in playing football. That was my first and last game. Picking myself up and assuring the guys, "Yeah, yeah, I'm okay, I'm okay," I thanked them for letting me play and hobbled off the field.

The football game reminded me that I can't do everything. Nor do I want to do everything. Who of us can or does? Some of us will excel at playing football, others at crocheting afghans, tending a garden, using computers, playing the guitar, fixing cars, building homes, doing research, teaching first grade. The secret of life is finding out (the earlier the better, but it's never too late) those things we can do and we like to do. Then, discovering how we can do these things to help make the world a better place.

God, lead me to discern those things I can and like to do; and show how I may use them in the service of others.

✿ ✿ ✿

149) Is order heaven's first law?

We hear a lot about the importance of order. "I've got to get more organized!" many of us scream when we can't find something. "I need more order in my life!" we cry when we're running late for something.

Alexander Pope said, "Order is heaven's first law." But is it? Is order really that high on God's list of priorities? Some evidence suggests, "Yes." Just look at creation and see all those planets circling the sun in an orderly fashion, or those four seasons following one another neatly. Look at the highly organized, molecular structure of things, too—everything. And what about those Ten Commandments? Aren't they just a list of ten ways to maintain order in our lives and in society?

Yes, there's some evidence to suggest that God likes order. But there's more evidence that says order is not God's top priority, let alone God's first law.

Just look at Jesus. Jesus was not a highly organized person. Throughout the gospels, he is shown coming and going, and going and coming—often in what appears to be a haphazard way. He is extremely flexible, allowing all kinds of individuals to come to him at will: Nicodemus, the ten lepers, Jairus, the blind man, a Roman centurion, to name a few. His apostles are the ones who seek more order. They want to shoo away the little children, for example. (Kids and order don't go together: just ask any new parent!) And his apostles are shocked to find Jesus conversing with a woman at the well, because they know (as everyone knows) a woman's place is in the home!

On numerous occasions, Jesus speaks out against order—or, more specifically, against allowing order to usurp the place of more important values, most notably love. Jesus says, for example, if you're on the way to the Temple to offer sacrifice and you suddenly remember you are at odds with someone, leave your sacrifice at the altar (surely not an orderly thing to do!) and go make amends with that person (Mt 5:23–24). The orderly person might object: "But first things first! That means God first, my neighbor second." But Jesus is saying, "Don't you see? Life's not that orderly! What you do to God, you do to your neighbor—and vice versa!" And when Jesus lambasts the scribes and Pharisees, he's really lambasting them for their deification of order, their way of organizing everyone into "them" and "us."

Finally, Jesus himself becomes a victim of order. He is put to death primarily because the "powers that be" feel he is a serious threat to the established order—both ecclesiastical and political.

All of this is not to say that order is not necessary. It is. In fact, order can even be commendable, but only if it serves other more important values—most notably, love.

Jesus, may I never make order my top priority.

✿ ✿ ✿

150) A horse named Lucky

It was Sunday afternoon when I got the call. It was Deanna, a girl in my freshman religion class. She was crying. "What's wrong?" I asked with concern. Through her sobs she told me, "Sister...my horse...Lucky...he's dead!"

I knew about Lucky. He was the young horse Deanna's parents had gotten for her earlier that year. She loved that horse, caring for him with devotion and riding him with pride.

"What happened?" I asked earnestly. Slowly, Deanna described what had happened: riding Lucky at the track that morning...someone else leading him back to the barn...the mud...the slip...the fall...the broken leg...the agonizing decision to have him put down.

I told Deanna how sorry I was. And, more importantly, I let her talk and cry. At one point she asked, "Sister, how could God let this happen?" I gave her the only answer I knew, the only real answer: "I don't know." And we spoke on about the beauty of horses, the sacredness of life, the mystery of death, and the inscrutability of God's ways. We didn't use those words, of course, but that certainly was the gist of our conversation.

I have always known how privileged I am to be a teacher. Moments like this one with Deanna, make me think, "Maybe lucky is a better word."

God, help me to realize how lucky I am to have you and other people in my life.

151) An alternate perception

I'm a morning person. As such, I sometimes do my grocery shopping quite early in the day, thus avoiding the crowds. I shared this practice with a friend of mine, a night owl. "When you go shopping at 7:00 in the morning, there are no lines at the checkout," I said proudly.

My friend grinned and said, "Melannie, there are no lines at the checkout at midnight, either!"

I had to laugh. For here I was, gloating over my discovery—and presuming that, by being a morning person, I somehow had an advantage over my friend. But she was quick to inform me: being a night owl gave her certain advantages, too.

The incident reminded me of these truths: no one has the complete picture. No one has the definitive perspective on life. We all need one another. Each of us can learn something from someone else—especially from those whose viewpoint is considerably different from our own.

Broadening our perspective on life is no small thing. Rather, it lies at the core of our Christian faith. For what are faith, hope, and love except alternate perceptions?

God, keep altering my perception of reality!

152) Lent and the process of repenting

When we think of Lent, we think of the words of John the Baptist: "Repent, for the kingdom of heaven has come near!" (Mt 3:2). Repent. What does that word mean? It means, first of all, to feel regret for something. "I'm sorry I broke your truck," we said (or were made to say!) to our little brother. "I'm sorry I got ketchup all over your blouse," we said to our teenage sister.

But repentance goes beyond expressing sorrow. Our little brother, holding his truck in two pieces, has a right to ask, "What are you going to do about this?" So does our teenage sister, holding up her ruined blouse.

Repentance goes beyond being sorry. To repent means to turn from sin and dedicate oneself to the amendment of one's life. Repentance, then, demands action. It demands change. But we're not talking surface change here—a new haircut, braces, losing ten pounds. No, we're talking serious change, deep change.

In an article entitled, "Turning Over a New Leaf," Robert Stoudt distinguishes between change and renewal. He writes, "Change pertains to exterior details, renewal to interiority." He goes on to say that change relates to "specific behaviors modified, curbed, or adapted"; whereas renewal "considers the suspect motivations that produce the behaviors in the first place."

A good question to reflect on during Lent, then, is this: what motivations are producing the behaviors I would like to change or modify? Fear? Hurt? Anger? Guilt? Getting to the motivational roots of my behaviors may take time. It may require help, too. But Lent offers us forty days to at least begin the process of repenting.

God, help me to identify the motivations that produce the behaviors I wish to change. And give me the strength to change them.

⚘ ⚘ ⚘

153) The writing lesson

Good morning, class! Today we're going to learn one of the secrets of good writing: good verbs.

Now we all know what a verb is, right? You don't remember? Then let's read what our book says a verb is: "A verb is a word that characteristically is the grammatical center of a predicate and expresses an act, occurrence, or mode of being that in various languages is inflected for agreement with the subject for tense, voice, or mood."

Now, who can tell me what that means? No one? Then I'll tell you. It means a verb is a word that conveys action or being, and changes all the time. Therefore, come and go, is and seems, love and hate, gargle and pirouette are all verbs—that is, unless they are being used as nouns. But that's a whole other lesson which we're not going to get into today. Today we're just going to talk about good writing, which means choosing good verbs.

Now, what do I mean when I say good verbs? No, I am not implying that some verbs are morally bad. Verbs are never morally bad even when they do awful things like lie, cheat, punch, kill, or even mutilate. That's not the verb's fault. That's their subjects' fault. No, when I say good verbs I mean verbs that are not worn out from overuse, like is, was, come, go, and even love, which is one of the most exhausted verbs in our entire language because people are using it all the time, saying things like "I love…" and finishing their sentences with everything from God to pickles! Poor love! What a workout it gets.

But good verbs are good verbs because they do more than describe an action. They paint a picture of that action. They help us see it. Let's look at an example. Here's a sentence: "Oscar came into the room." Simple. Clear. Grammatically correct. But compare that sentence to this one: "Oscar hobbled into the room." The verb "hobble" not only tells you that Oscar came into the room, it also tells you how he came into the room: hobbling. Now that's a good verb!

What are some other good verbs we could have used in that sentence? That's right: shuffled, danced, crawled, ran, slithered, pranced, strolled, scampered, floated, ambled, drifted, sauntered, barged, meandered, tip-toed…okay, okay. You get the point.

Now, I am not saying that there's only one right verb for every sentence, and we'd better choose it, or else. No, as in life, our choice often is not between a bad verb and a good verb, but between two good verbs. How do we pick one, you ask? Perhaps we consult the dictionary to see if there are some subtle differences between the two. Other times we choose one because it just sounds right, it fits better.

Experience, coupled with sensitivity, helps us to make good choices when it comes to verbs. Come to think of it, experience and sensitivity help us to make good choices when it comes to anything. (RING!!!) There's the bell! I guess that's all for today, class. Don't forget: good writing, good verbs! See you tomorrow!

God, help me to make good choices today.

154) Hummingbirds

I phone my mother to wish her a happy Mother's Day. "Guess what?" she says to me with excitement. Before I can even proffer a guess, she tells me. "Our hummingbirds are back!"

My parents have lived for over fifteen years on three plus acres in semi-rural northeastern Ohio. And every May, they religiously hang a hummingbird feeder outside their kitchen window. And every May, the hummingbirds, just as religiously, show up. From the excitement in my mother's voice, I know the arrival of the hummingbirds is an event worthy of celebration.

I admire hummingbirds! First, they're so tiny—not much larger than a bumblebee. Second, they go so fast! Even a slow motion camera can't capture their rapidly beating wings. Third, they fly in any direction: up, down, frontwards, backwards, sideways. As far as I know, no other bird rivals them in agility. (Every time I'm at an airport and see an airplane being pushed back from the gate, I think, "Our airplanes are sure klutzy compared to God's hummingbirds!")

Another reason hummingbirds intrigue me is their beauty: those flitting iridescent colors that poet Emily Dickinson describes as "A resonance of emerald,/ A rush of cochineal." But perhaps I admire hummingbirds most because of their ability to migrate thousands of miles on less than an ounce of fat. And some, I've heard, actually fly across the Gulf of Mexico in one stretch!

The secret of the hummingbirds' aeronautical capabilities, of course, is that they, like almost all birds, travel light. (I've yet to see any bird flying south with a suitcase dangling from its leg!) Maybe that's one of the messages God speaks to us through humming-birds and other birds. (God speaks another message through ostriches and emus!) It's a message we pack rats, junk collectors, and gizmo addicts need to hear more than once: travel light. Travel light. Or, as Jesus himself said, "Do not store up for yourselves trea-sures on earth…but store up for yourselves treasures in heaven…. For where your treasure is, there your heart will be also" (Mt 6:19–21).

God, help me to travel light.

⁊* ⁊* ⁊*

155) Quotes on opportunity

Opportunities are seldom labeled. (Claude McDonald)

When one door closes, another opens; but we often look so long and so regretfully upon the closed door, we do not see the one which has opened before us. (Alexander Graham Bell)

There is no security on this earth; there is only opportunity. (General Douglas MacArthur)

Sometimes opportunity knocks, but most of the time it sneaks up on you and then quietly steals away. (Doug Larson)

Great opportunities to help others seldom come, but small ones surround us every day. (Sally Kock)

*God, open my eyes to the small opportunities that surround
me today.*

✸ ✸ ✸

156) The beckoning risen Jesus

Many Christians probably prefer Christmas to Easter. That's understandable, for the Christmas story has many elements that are naturally attractive: a newborn baby, a young married couple, a mys-
terious star, woolly sheep, angelic choirs, and a motley group of
shepherds who end up with the best seats in the house.

In contrast, what does Easter have to offer? A stone rolled back,
an empty tomb, and three women running madly, scared out of
their wits. Another way of looking at the two feasts is this: at
Christmas, we say "hello" to Jesus; but at Easter we say "goodbye."
For, in a way, Easter is about "parting company," about Jesus parting company with us. For, when he rose from the dead, Jesus did
not simply come back from the dead. He was not merely resusci-
tated. No, when he rose, he went beyond death to an intrinsically
new life. And it is from there that he beckons us to come and be
with him.

Of course, in one sense, Jesus is always here with us, yes. But in
a deeper way, he goes before us. That's what Easter proclaims. "He
is not here," the angel says to the women. "He is going ahead of
you" (Mt 28:6–7). And it is imperative that we keep before us that
image of a beckoning risen Jesus. Why? So we never succumb to
the temptation to look for salvation "back there" or in "the way
things used to be." So we never get too cozy in the present and fail
to hear the cries of the poor all around us. So that we never make
the mistake of thinking we are already home, but rather, we are on
a journey toward home.

Risen Jesus, keep beckoning me!

157) Easter surprises

If there's one word that summarizes Easter, it's the word, "Surprise!" All four evangelists, while emphasizing different aspects of the Easter story, all make one thing clear: Jesus' resurrection was a big surprise not only for his enemies, but even for his closest followers.

In Mark, the three women who trek to the tomb early Sunday morning are astonished and frightened when they find the tomb empty (Mk 16:1–8). In Matthew, even when the disciples see the risen Jesus with their own eyes, they still doubt that it is really he, so startled are they by his appearance (Mt 28:17). In Luke, the two disciples on the way to Emmaus are flabbergasted when they realize that the guy who nonchalantly joined them on their walk was actually the risen Jesus (Lk 24:13–32). And in John, Mary Magdalene doesn't have a clue that the man in the garden is Jesus until he surprises her by calling her name (Jn 20:11–18).

One fitting way to celebrate Easter, then, is to surprise people. We can begin by surprising ourselves, by doing something we don't ordinarily do. If we never read short stories, we might read one. If we've never eaten tofu, we could try it. The options are almost unlimited: we could write a poem, sign up for a pottery class, play cards, go dancing, visit an art museum, work on our family tree, buy a hibiscus plant. What's the point of surprising ourselves during the Easter season? It is one way for us to get out of our rut or (if you will) out of our "tomb," that is, our usual way of doing things. Surprising ourselves is one way for us to grow, to be enlivened, and to stretch beyond where we are. What an Easter kind of thing to do!

We can also celebrate Easter by surprising others, by doing small favors around the house, the workplace, the parish, the neighborhood. We can surprise individuals with phone calls or visits or by sending notes or postcards for no particular occasion.

Someone has said, "The simplest meaning of Easter is that we are living in a world in which God has the last word." That last word may very well be "Surprise!"

Jesus, help me to surprise myself and someone else today.

✿ ✿ ✿

158) A religious person

Ellie is a young single mother who lives next door to me with her ten-month-old baby, Bryan. She stops in with Bryan every now and then to visit me. One time the three of us were sitting on my living room floor together. (Babies have an uncanny way of making me willingly forgo the comfort and dignity of a living room chair!)

"So," says Ellie as Bryan jumps up and down in her arms. "What kind of stuff do you write?"

I reply, "Mostly educational and religious things."

"Religious things?" she asks letting Bryan go.

"Yeah. You know, scripture and prayer. Stuff like that."

Ellie continues, "I'm not a religious person," she says. "But sometimes I'll be sitting on the living room floor playing with Bryan, and all of a sudden I'll just say in my heart, 'Thank you, God, for giving me this beautiful, healthy baby boy!'"

Later that evening, I reflected on Ellie's words: "I'm not a religious person." And I thought, "Yes, you are, Ellie! Yes you are!"

For that's precisely what it means to be a religious person. It doesn't mean (necessarily) going to church, reciting formal prayers, reading spiritual books, and performing acts of piety. It means exactly what Ellie had unknowingly described—the fundamental religious act of saying "thank you" to one's deity.

That night, before crawling into bed, I thanked God for giving me such good neighbors!

God, thank you for _____.

159) Funeral plans

I know a number of people who have planned their own funerals. They've chosen the songs, picked a homilist, and even designed the cover for their program. These folks are not seriously ill, mind you. Most of them are in the prime of life, enjoying good health, and, barring no accidents, are likely to live several more decades.

I, for one, have not the slightest inclination to plan my own funeral. And it's not because I think such a thing is macabre or sick. Nor is it because I'm afraid to face the inevitability of my own death. No, I refuse to plan my funeral for one basic reason, a reason rooted in this fundamental question: who is the funeral for, anyway?

Some might say the funeral is for the funeralee, that is, the one being buried. But I ask, is it really? What need does the deceased have for a funeral? He or she is dead! Strictly speaking, the deceased has need of nothing we living can give anymore (except perhaps a prayer or two). In fact, a good definition of being dead is just that: having no more earthly needs, which includes no need for a funeral. So, when I think of planning my own, I say to myself, "*What for*?? It's not going to matter to you! Nothing's going to matter to you once you're dead!" (Such a thought, far from filling me with alarm, fills me with elation!)

I am suggesting, then, that funerals are primarily for the mourners. These are the people left behind in sorrow and pain. They're the ones who need all the consolation they can get, and they can get some of that consolation by planning and celebrating their loved one's funeral. All those beautiful songs, all those consoling scripture readings, all those powerful prayers for them to choose from.

If, after reading this, you still feel compelled to plan your own funeral, then, by all means, go ahead. But I, for one, have irrevocably crossed it off of my list of "Things to do before I die" (my list is already too long).

God, give me a healthy awareness of the inevitability of my own death. And may that awareness influence my choices today.

160) The parable of the Last Judgment

The parable of the Last Judgment (Mt 25:31–46) is a sobering one. In it, Jesus is shown dividing a gigantic herd of people into two groups: the sheep (whom he directs to his right) and the goats (to his left). Then Jesus says to the sheep, "Come, you that are blessed by my Father, inherit the kingdom prepared for you from the foundation of the world." The sheep are shocked. "Who—*us*?" they ask. It is clear they haven't a clue what they did to deserve this.

So Jesus tells them: "I was hungry...thirsty...a stranger... naked...sick...in prison...and you cared for me." The sheep are amazed. "But we never saw you," they protest. Then Jesus says those beautiful words, "Just as you did it to one of the least of these...you did it to me."

Then Jesus turns to the goats and says (in a nutshell), "You never cared for me when I was in need." The goats object, "But when did we see you in need?" To which Jesus says those somber words, "Just as you did not do it to one of the least of these, you did not do it to me."

Recently a friend, preaching on this passage, said, "The question we must ask ourselves is this: 'Where am I missing Jesus today?'" I'd modify that slightly: "In whom am I missing Jesus today?" In other words, in what person or persons do I think Jesus isn't today? That elderly woman with Alzheimer's? That newborn baby with AIDS? That lawyer with his briefcase? That man on death row? That bishop in his miter? That young mother on welfare? Those radicals? Those terrorists? Those women? Those gays?

Where is Jesus today for me? Probably in the person I least expect.

Jesus, give me eyes to see you in the people I least expect.

🌱 🌱 🌱

161) "I want to want!"

Shortly before Eric's sixth birthday, his grandmother asked him, "Eric, what do you need for your birthday?" Eric wrinkled up his nose and replied emphatically, "I don't want to need! I want to want!"

Though not even six, Eric already knew there's a difference between "need" and "want." "Need" is what you have to have—like underwear, toothpaste, green vegetables. No fun there. But "want" is what you'd like to have, and that opens up a whole world of unlimited possibilities—like roller blades, video games, chocolate candy bars!

Spiritual writers tell us we must distinguish between our needs and our wants, between those things essential for living and those things that aren't. Good advice, especially for those of us living in a so-called consumer society. For our consumer society works overtime trying to convince us that all our wants are really needs. It has succeeded in doing this every time we say (or think) things like this: "I have to have that _____!" (Fill in the blank with dress, car, computer, chain saw, stereo, ring, lawn mower, vacation, exercise machine, book, boat, gizmo, gadget, or anything else you can think of.)

There's a danger in focusing too much on satisfying only our wants. If we do, life becomes little more than a frantic and frenzied pursuit for more and more things. Simultaneously, such a preoccupation distracts us from ever discovering and exploring our deeper and far more vital needs—like our need for intimacy, solitude, truth, leisure, forgiveness, love—and even our need for God.

God, lead me to discover my deepest needs, especially my need for you.

℣ ℣ ℣

162) Quilting: "That's what piecing is"

In her 1991 Madeleva Lecture in Spirituality, Dolores Leckey focuses on "Women and Creativity." She speaks of the many pioneer women who designed and sewed all those incredibly beautiful quilts. Leckey notes that, to these women, quilting was not only "an artistic statement," it was also "a philosophical expression." She cites the words of an elderly quilter found in the book *The Quilters: Women and Domestic Art, An Oral History*. The woman begins by describing life on the frontier, and ends up talking about quilting as if living and quilting were one and the same thing. I'll quote her, bad grammar and all:

> Sometimes you don't have control over the way things go....And then you're given just so much to work with in life and you have to do the best you can with what you got. That's what piecing is. The materials is passed on to you or is all you can afford to buy...your fate. But the way you put them together is your business. You can put them in any order you like.

In a way, living is quilting. We start with those scraps of material passed on to us—our genetic makeup, our family history, our upbringing. Then we purchase other materials we can afford to buy with the talents and opportunities we've been given. And finally, we take all those pieces of material and we put them together. In any order we like. In a unique pattern of our own making. That's what piecing is. That's what piecing a life is!

God, help me piece together a beautiful life for you.

⚘ ⚘ ⚘

163) Draw what you see

When I took biology in high school, we periodically examined things under the microscope—things like an amoeba, a strand of hair, a leaf, a drop of blood. Sometimes the teacher would say to us, "Draw what you see." Inevitably, sooner or later one of us would ask, "What's it supposed to look like?" The question always irked our teacher, who'd say something like, "Forget what it's supposed to look like and draw what you see!" But even then, some of us would peek in our textbook, find a picture of what we were looking at, and copy that picture!

There's something in us that makes us fearful of trusting our own experience. Maybe, over the years, we've made some big mistakes or gotten seriously burned by doing just that. In addition, the church herself sometimes fostered this attitude of mistrust when she overemphasized "people as sinners" and the world as "the world"—which meant they were both, if not intrinsically evil, than downright questionable and, therefore, shouldn't be trusted. Many people feel that it is far safer to trust the experience of other people—the so-called "experts" like the saints, the pope, priests, theologians, spiritual writers, psychologists, and the like. Consequently, many of us find ourselves running to these people and frantically asking, "What's life supposed to look like, feel like, and mean, anyway? What's God supposed to be like?" instead of considering our own experience, instead of drawing what we see.

I am not saying we shouldn't ask advice, seek counsel, or read books (like this one)—heavens, no! The experience of others can lead, guide, and enrich us. (In one sense, that's precisely what the church is for—to lead and guide. That's also my hope for a book like this—that it will enrich.) But the experience of others is never a substitute for our own. In fact, another's experience helps us only if it somehow illuminates our own experience. And this will happen only if we are in touch with our own experience.

Why is it so important to consider and reflect on our own experience, that is, to draw what we see? Because, as the saints have taught over the centuries, that's primarily where we encounter God—in the experiences of our everyday lives.

God, help me to seek and find you in my own experience,

and to draw what I see.

✿ ✿ ✿

164) The deer principle

For five years I lived on a 180-acre estate in Middleburg, Virginia. We Sisters of Notre Dame owned a school there, right in the middle of Virginia's famed horse country. Picture it: towering magnolia trees, rolling green pastures, thick woods, blue mountains to the west, and a driveway nine-tenths of a mile long! A lover of the outdoors, I frequently took long walks on our property. Sometimes I would spot deer along the way—usually in clumps of three or four, but occasionally even in herds of a dozen or more.

My walks amid all that beauty taught me many things. One thing I call "the deer principle." And it goes like this. Whenever I set out deliberately to see deer, I seldom saw them. But if, on the other hand, I was just strolling along with my mind on other things, *presto*! there they'd be! Silent, statuesque, and staring right at me. It was as if as soon as I let go of my resolve to see deer, they would oblige me with their presence!

I've experienced "the deer principle" in other areas of my life as well. Take writing. I, for one, work hard at writing—at coming up with ideas, finding the right words, and organizing what I have to say. But, I must confess, sometimes I am most creative not when I am most alert and most in control, but when I am half-asleep with the reins of the day slipping out of my hands. This occurs most noticeably twice a day: those few minutes before I fall asleep at night and (even more so) before I am fully awake in the morning. Those times I am no longer desperately trying to make something happen. As soon as I let go, *presto*! all kinds of ideas, images and words suddenly appear. (In fact, the idea for this reflection came to me as I lay in bed one morning.)

Does the "deer principle" apply to our spiritual lives as well? I say, "Yes!" We go to prayer saying things like, "I will meet God today! I will find an answer to my question! I will come up with a solution to this problem!" And what happens? Nothing! But later during the day or during the week, when we're taking a shower or stirring the chili or playing with the dog, *presto!* God's there, silent, statuesque, and gazing at us with amusement and affection.

God, teach me how to let go and allow you to oblige me with your presence.

165) Humorous observations about sundry items

Getting caught is the mother of invention. (Robert Byrne)

Why is it we trust banks with our money and they don't trust us with their pens? (Anonymous)

Stephen Spender, describing the face of W.H. Auden: "A wedding cake left out in the rain."

The nice thing about egotists is that they don't talk about other people. (Lucille Harper)

Running is an unnatural act—except from enemies and to the bathroom. (Anonymous)

He who laughs, lasts. (Mary Pettibone Poole)

God, keep me laughing—to the last!

166) The spirituality of wishing

Five-year-old Timmy was touring the Luray Caverns in Virginia with his parents. At the end of the tour, they came to a crystal-clear pool of water. "This is our wishing pond," announced the guide. Timmy begged his father for some coins. Taking them, he threw them into the pond and cried aloud, "I wish for a thousand toys!"

As the family exited the caverns, Timmy suddenly appeared worried and anxious. "What's wrong?" his father asked. He replied somberly, "Where am I gonna put all those toys?"

Wishing is something we learn to do quite early in life. And with good reason, for wishing is very important for our psychological well-being. Healthy wishing enables us to move beyond the past and the present. It spurs us to set goals for the future, and encourages us to use our time and talents to work toward their achievement.

Wishing is also important for our spiritual well-being. It puts us in touch with our incompleteness by reminding us we are never fully satisfied with who we are, what we have, and the way things are going. And this is good. For every wish bears the seed for improvement. And every wish attests to our need for God.

Healthy wishing, though, is never made in isolation. It always takes into consideration the wishes of others. Otherwise, wishing degenerates into selfishness. Healthy wishing must also be coupled with action. Otherwise, it is feckless daydreaming. If we wish to get a college degree, for example, we must take steps to achieve that goal. If we wish to end world hunger, we must take steps (no matter how small) to work toward that aim, for example, educating ourselves, examining our consumer practices, helping to influence legislation, and so on.

Jesus said, "Where your treasure is, there your heart will also be" (Lk 12:34). Similarly, we could say, "Where your wishing is, there you heart is." To get a spiritual EKG, we need only ask ourselves: "What am I wishing for?"

God, may all my wishes lead to improvement—and to you!

167) It all depends on angle and framing

Today I took a picture of a small, shapely pine tree enveloped in the morning mist. It took me quite some time to take the picture. I knew what I wanted (an up-shot), but when I stooped to take it from that angle, I kept getting some telephone lines in the picture. Not wanting them in, I began to adjust my position—now to the left, back a little to the right, now a little lower, now a little closer—until, "*Yes!* That's it!" And I snapped the picture.

Taking pictures always reminds me that the whole effect of the final picture rests largely on these two components: angle and framing. A good photographer is always asking, "What's the best angle to take this from? What do I intentionally wish to include and exclude?"

In life, much depends on angle and framing, too. When annoyed or disturbed by something, we can ask ourselves, "From what angle am I viewing this person, this thing, this situation?" Perhaps if I changed my point of view, I would see something I'm not seeing now. And, "What am I framing here?" Maybe there's something I should leave out of the picture, or something I should include that I'm not.

God, make me more aware of angle and framing today. Help me get your picture.

※ ※ ※

168) Our image of the truth

St. Julie Billiart founded the Sisters of Notre Dame in post-revolutionary France. Reading her letters, one realizes she had more than her share of problems. One problem involved some of the clergy of her day who sometimes opposed Julie and her fledgling congregation. One day Julie received a letter from one of her sisters describing how a priest had yelled at her with considerable rage. Julie wrote back, "Even though he were to shout so loudly that I could hear him from here, that good priest would not frighten me....Truth does not make so much noise."

Julie was on to something when she said, "Truth does not make so much noise." What do I mean? To answer that, we first have to ask, what exactly is truth? It's a word we use almost glibly today. "We print only the truth!" boasts the newspaper tabloid. "Do you swear to tell the truth?" the bailiff asks the court witness. "Now, Johnny, tell the truth," the mother urges her naughty child. The question, "What is truth?" is a formidable one. Little wonder, then, we shy away from trying to answer it. But there's another question, less overwhelming perhaps, but no less important, that we might want to explore: what is our *image* of the truth? For our image of the truth may hold the key to what truth really is.

Is our image of the truth the blast of a thousand trumpets or the soft strains of a single flute? Is it a flashy display of fireworks or the steady flicker of a lone candle? Is truth a raging hurricane or a gentle but unfaltering breeze? A volcano erupting high into the air or a seed cracking open in the soil?

Shortly before handing Jesus over to be crucified, Pilate asks him, "What is truth?" (Jn 18:38). In response to his question, Pilate doesn't get a lengthy dissertation or an impressive display of military might. He doesn't even get a halfway decent little miracle. Instead Pilate gets silence. Only silence. But, as someone has wisely pointed out, "There are times when nothing a person can say is so powerful as saying nothing." For the ultimate answer to Pilate's "What is truth?" is not a philosophical concept or major event; it is a person, the person standing before him: Jesus, "The way, and the truth, and the life" (Jn 14:6).

St. Julie was right: Truth doesn't make so much noise. He doesn't have to.

Jesus, continue to lead me to truth which (I know) is ultimately you.

✲ ✲ ✲

169) Happiness

Happiness attracts. We enter a room filled with people, and toward whom do we gravitate? That's right, toward those folks over there who are laughing a lot. We go out to dinner with a group, and whom do we try to sit next to? Yes, that person with a good sense of humor. We have a choice of clerks at the service desk of the discount store. Which one do we choose? Probably the one with the smile.

Yes, happiness attracts. Even when we're not feeling particularly happy ourselves, we may seek out happy individuals to be with, hoping (I suppose) that some of their happiness rubs off on us.

But sometimes happiness repels. Sometimes we may be so miserable, we find it hard to see someone else who is happy. When this occurs, we may find ourselves thinking things like this:

"If she had to suffer like I have to suffer, she wouldn't be so doggone cheerful!"

"He's happy now, but just wait until life deals him a few hard blows—like it's dealt me!"

"She's a very shallow person. Anyone that happy has to be!"

One indication of how healthy our Christian spirituality is, obviously, our own level of happiness. After all, Jesus said, "Happy are those who hear the word of God and keep it" (Lk 11:28). But an even more reliable indicator is this: our ability to delight in the happiness of others, even when we ourselves may be experiencing pain.

God, teach me to delight in another's happiness today.

✲ ✲ ✲

170) On going to bed at night

Sometimes I think the way we go to bed at night is the way we're going to go to our death. If we go to bed fussing and stalling and puttering and refusing to leave our work, that's how we'll die: fussing and stalling and puttering and refusing to leave this world. I hope my little theory is correct, for I, for one, usually go to bed quite readily, perfectly content to leave some things left unfinished. I tell myself as I crawl beneath the covers, "I'll pick up tomorrow where I left off today." I hope I'm just as ready and eager to die when the time comes: No fussing. No stalling. No regrets. No frets about leaving some things undone.

In fact, I hope when it's time for me to die, I can say: "What, God? It's time for me to go? Why, sure! I'll be right with you. After all, I've been expecting you!" Or, "You're a little earlier than I planned, God, but that's okay. I'm ready." Or, "It's about time you got here, God! What took you so long?"

God, help me to realize that I prepare for my death by how I live my life every day.

⚘ ⚘ ⚘

171) Quotes from obscure sources

Being bored is a sin against gratitude. (Melannie Svoboda, SND)

God continuously offers us life, but we have to say "yes" to God's offer. And the problem is, saying "yes" can look a lot like dying. (Sister Melannie Svoboda)

The applause of a room full of strangers is not worth the clap of a single friend. (Melannie Svoboda)

What fascinates me the most in a person is whether he or she seems fascinated by me. (Mel Svoboda)

Whether I'm having a good day or a bad day, I always remind myself: I'm on my way to a better place! (S.M. Svoboda)

God, help me to remember to keep you in front of me at all times.

ᴙ⁕ ᴙ⁕ ᴙ⁕

172) Sloth

The cartoon shows two elderly monks walking together. One says to the other, "At my age, sloth is the only sin I've got left!"

Whatever happened to the sin of sloth? It certainly is not a sin we read much about these days. In the book of Proverbs, on the other hand, we find frequent mention of the sin of sloth, sometimes called "laziness" or "idleness": "As a door turns on its hinges, so does a lazy person in bed" (Prv 26:14); "One who is slack in work is close kin to a vandal" (Prv 18:9); "The hand of the diligent will rule, while the lazy will be put to forced labor" (Prv 12:24); and, "Go to the ant, you lazybones; consider its ways, and be wise" (Prv 6:6).

Strictly speaking, the word "sloth" means more than mere laziness or idleness. It is far more dangerous, too. Sloth is really the sin of "acedia," which the fourth-century Christian ascetics dubbed "the noonday devil." According to theology professor Louis Cameli, acedia tempts us in three ways. First, it tempts us to return to the past, our former way of life, the way things used to be. The Israelites in the desert, for example, pined for the fleshpots of Egypt as soon as their journey became difficult (Ex 16:2–3). Secondly, acedia tempts us to do something other than what we have been called to do. For example, I've known some parents who get so involved in their parish, they end up neglecting their own children! And thirdly, acedia tempts us "to collapse into paralyzing sadness at the futility of it all," "it" being whatever good we are trying to do. Acedia whispers in our ear, "What's the use? You're only one person. Give it up already!"

Sloth or acedia can tempt individuals as well as communities. Look around, for it is still very much alive in our world today. Perhaps it's even nesting in our own hearts.

God, help me to continue on my journey, to do what you are calling me to do, and to never succumb to despair.

⚘ ⚘ ⚘

173) Jesus: Prince of Peace or Agitation?

Jesus is called the Prince of Peace. That is the name given him by the prophet Isaiah long before his birth: "And he is named Wonderful Counselor, Mighty God, Everlasting Father, Prince of Peace" (Is 9:6). Peace is what Jesus wishes his apostles, too, at the Last Supper: "Peace I leave with you; my peace I give to you" (Jn 14:27). It is also the first word he speaks to his anxious apostles after his resurrection: "Peace be with you" (Lk 24:36). Yet, in other places, Jesus specifically warns his followers against associating him exclusively with peace. "Do not think that I have come to bring peace to the earth" (Mt 10:34), he says. He then goes on to describe some of the possible unpeaceful consequences of believing in him—most notably, turmoil and conflicts in familial relationships.

Jesus is our Prince of Peace—but not exclusively that. He is sometimes also our Prince of Agitation. Let me explain.

To begin with, peace is not an absolute good. It can be a good, certainly, but sometimes it can be a cop-out or (worse yet) an abettor to evil. For example, we see a friend doing something very wrong or harmful, and we say, "I'd say something, but I don't want to get him upset." In other words, we choose peace rather than honesty or genuine love. Or we see a blatant injustice and say, "I'd do something about that, but I don't want to cause a fuss." Translation? "Peace at any price—even at the price of truth and goodness."

Literature promotes the notion that too much peace is not good for us. Take the magnificent poem *The Rime of the Ancient Mariner*, by Samuel Taylor Coleridge. In that poem, a mighty sailing vessel gets caught in a terrible storm. Petrified, the sailors pray for relief from the violence and turmoil. Eventually, their prayer seems to be answered as their ship is blown into a perfectly peaceful sea. At first they are overjoyed. Peace at last! Calm after all that tumult! Only gradually do the men realize that this calm is no blessing at all. In fact, it means certain death for all of them. Their ship, "As idle as a painted ship/Upon a painted ocean," is stuck. It is going nowhere. They will all die.

In sailing, absolute peace and calm mean death. In the spiritual life, it is the same way. That's why Jesus, on a regular basis, comes into our lives as the Prince of Agitation, stirring our waters, ruffling our feathers, messing up our ordered lives, goading us to sail on.

Jesus, make me more sensitive to your presence in my life— whether you come as Prince of Peace or Agitation.

⚘ ⚘ ⚘

174) Taking time for the pain

There's an old song I like with a line that says, "I haven't got time for the pain." (The song was eventually used in an aspirin commercial!) The words are those of someone who has recently experienced the pain of a broken relationship. What the song is saying is this: "I'm putting the pain of this experience behind me in order to get on with my life."

In one way, the words of the song are wise. We cannot let the pain of the past prevent us from living in the present and moving on into the future. But in another way, the words are dangerous if they are saying we should ignore our pain. On the contrary, it is very important for us to take time for our pain. How do we do this? By getting in touch with our pain and openly admitting it to ourselves and perhaps to someone else in whom we can confide. Why do we do this? So we can decide where our pain is going to take us— toward more self-pity, resentment, or violence? Or will our pain lead us to greater understanding, compassion, forgiveness, love?

In James Baldwin's book *Notes of a Native Son*, we find these insightful words: "I imagine one of the reasons people cling to their hates so stubbornly is because they sense, once hate is gone, they will be forced to deal with pain." Dealing with pain is never easy. But if we don't, the consequences can be devastating—for ourselves and for our world.

God, help me to take time for my pain. And may it always lead me to greater understanding and love.

175) Babies: one of God's greatest ideas

One of God's best ideas was babies. Just think of it. All human beings, no matter what century they're born in, no matter what race, gender, or religion, all start out in life the same way: as babies. It didn't have to be that way. God could have had all of us, like the Greek goddess Athena, spring full grown from our mother's (or father's) head. Or we all could have hatched from giant eggs at the age of twenty-one. But no. God decided all human beings would begin their earthly journey as babies—as tiny, fidgeting, cooing, screaming, drooling, defenseless babies. Why?

I don't know why. But I can speculate. For one thing, babies are lovable. I know, I know, babies aren't *always* lovable. Not when they cry at 3:00 in the morning, or wet their diaper (or worse), or spit carrots in your face, or drool on your best pair of pants. But despite the many unlovable things babies do, they somehow still remain lovable. Just take a baby anywhere—into a checkout line, into a church, onto a bus—and notice what happens. Immediately all heads turn. Some people instantly begin smiling or waving or saying "Aw!" or speaking in "babylese," you know, saying things like, "kitchie-coo." Babies would never elicit such positive responses if they weren't so doggone lovable, not to mention cute!

But there's another reason why I think God came up with the idea of babies. Babies need a heck of a lot of love. To begin with, they are absolutely dependent upon other human beings for their survival. Whereas the babies of other species of animals become independent quite soon after birth (like turtles, rabbits, and hedgehogs), we human babies require many years of careful nurturing just to get us to where we can cross the street by ourselves, let alone make a living!

This means as long as there are babies in the world, there's going to be a lot of loving going on. There has to be. And God probably thought that was a pretty good idea. Babies are one of the ways God came up with for reminding us how important love really is. And God didn't mean just for babies either. All human beings need a heck of a lot of love no matter what their age—babies, kids, teenagers, young adults, mid-lifers, or senior citizens. Paraphrasing the old motto of the dairy farmers, "We never outgrow our need for love."

Babies are a good way for God to impress upon all human beings the absolute necessity for love. In fact, God liked the idea of babies so much that, at one point, God made this incredibly remarkable, amazingly phenomenal, totally astonishing decision: "I, myself, will become a baby, too!"

God, help me to love everyone you put into my life today— regardless of their age!

⚘ ⚘ ⚘

INDEX

The numbers indicate the number of the reflection.

acceptance: 1, 42, 136, 162
addiction: 130
Advent: 101, 111
adversity: 34, 38, 40, 57, 73,
    109, 112, 173
aging: 35, 54, 144
anger: 10, 14
animals: 16, 34, 51, 65, 71,
    103, 127, 134, 140, 150,
    154,164
art: 125
attention: 20, 85, l64
attitude: (see also percep-
    tion): 17, 46, 85, 98, 151,
    167

babies: 175
beauty: 10, 29, 33
Bible (see scripture)
caring (see also love): 27,
    139, 175

change: 135, 136, 152
children: 2, 20, 25, 31, 37, 43,
    46, 82, 97, 125, 142, 161,
    175
Christmas: 111, 112, 113, 124,
    156
church: 49, 78, 83, 132
commitment: 3
community: 34, 78, 127, 128,
    136, 151
compassion (see love)

consumerism: 161
conversation: 45
conversion: 135
creativity: 125
criticism: 108

darkness: 93, 116
death: 25, 63, 70, 150, 159,
    170
desire (longing): 80, 101, 102,
    161, 165
detachment (see also letting
    go): 154, 164, 170
Dickinson, Emily: 15
discernment: 76, 85, 90, 148,
    153, 162, 164

Easter: 156, 157
ecumenism: 132
education (see also teaching):
    54, 55, 59, 150
enthusiasm: 2
Eucharist (see Mass)
evangelization: 45
experience: 15, 163

faith: 12, 22, 24, 31, 91, 96,
    98, 112, 141
family: 18
fear: 61, 71, 116, 139
forgiveness (see also reconcil-
    iation): 60, 64, 106, 147
freedom: 43

friendship: 31, 62, 68, 100, 109
fun: 19
funerals: 159
future: 61, 165

generativity: 141
God: 20, 56, 61, 64, 71, 109, 111, 120, 121, 132, 158, 164
gratitude: 28, 36, 55, 70, 72, 81, 87, 103, 134, 158
grief: 25

happiness: 8, 19, 48, 82, 169
heaven: 9, 63
Holy Spirit: 125
homilies: 123
honesty: 27
hope: 38, 67, 91
humility: 86, 122, 130, 147
humor: 24, 77, 107, 118, 166
hypocrisy: 122

imagination: 94

jealousy: 80
Jesus: 1, 6, 17, 29, 31, 32, 41, 44, 50, 60, 67, 74, 88, 98, 101, 110, 116, 156, 173
Joseph: 112
joy: 2, 19, 89
justice: 82, 90, 99, 128, 160

knowledge: 4, 15

Last Judgment: 160

laziness: 172
leisure: 76, 110, 131
Lent: 152
letting go: 23, 76, 164, 170
life: 3, 36, 55, 92, 133, 138, 150, 162
limitations: 15, 42, 43, 89, 116, 122, 162
liturgy (see Mass)
longing (see desire)
love: 6, 16, 18, 25, 27, 37, 50, 60, 64, 65, 70, 74, 82, 94, 108, 114, 115, 120, 125, 142, 145, 147, 149, 160, 175

Mary: 1, 32, 69, 104, 112
Mass (Eucharist): 5, 122, 123, 159
meaning: 133
mercy: 119, 122
ministry (service): 6, 41, 45, 46, 83, 131,
miracles: 36
morality: 114, 126, 137
music: 57

names: 118, 140
nature: 33, 34, 35, 43, 51, 55, 81, 103, 127, 134, 140
New Year's Day: 117
Nicodemus: 12

obedience: 29
opportunity: 155
order: 149
ordinary: 48

Our Father: 7

parenthood: 142
patience: 18, 69
peace: 173
perception/perspective: 69,
    85, 98, 100, 115, 126, 143,
    147, 151, 163, 167
perfection: 119
pleasure: 48, 66, 84
prayer: 1, 5, 7, 21, 32, 50, 56,
    69, 73, 75, 93, 99, 109,
    124, 131, 146, 147
priorities: 46, 85, 143, 149
procrastination: 52, 79
proverbs: 53

quilting: 162
quotes: 8, 22, 40, 53, 62, 72,
    95, 121, 138, 155, 171

reconciliation: 60, 106, 147
religion: 158
remember: 129
repentance: 106, 152
resolutions: 117
resurrection: 67, 156
retreat: 23

St. Valentine's Day: 121
sacrifice: 65, 136
saints: 18, 30, 66
scandal: 74
scripture (Bible) 26, 47, 123,

124, 125, 129
self-esteem: 13, 94, 105
sensitivity: 44, 127
service (see also love and
    ministry): 125, 131
sexuality: 84, 102, 126
silence: 146
sin: 11, 26, 126
sloth: 172
suffering (pain): 19, 38, 40,
    43, 46, 73, 82, 89, 109,
    112, 127, 150, 174
surprise: 157

talents: 42, 162
teaching (see also education):
    59, 150
trust: 31, 38, 61, 71, 73, 91,
    116, 130, 139, 144, 150,
    163, 170
truth: 108, 168

values: 143, 149

waiting: 52
wholeness: 119
wisdom: 15, 95
wishing: 165
wonder: 36, 51, 55, 137, 154
words: 39, 133, 153
work: 83, 110, 131
writing: 21, 39, 58, 92, 125,
    153

Other Titles by Sr. Melannie...

Rummaging for God
Seeking the Holy in Every Nook and Cranny

In her latest book, Sr. Melannie uses the image of rummaging to build a series of meditations of how to find God in everyday events. Each of these engaging and uplifting meditations concludes with pertinent questions and a closing prayer.

136 pp, $9.95 (order J-21)

Teaching Is Like...
Pealing Back Eggshells

The author suggests that a teacher is like a farmer helping young chicks to hatch by gently peeling back a portion of the eggshell so as to ease the birth (of new ideas for students). Warm and witty, these fifty reflections of an outstanding teacher will give catechists the boost they need to continue the important task of being an effective, enthusiastic teacher.

120 pp, $7.95 (order M-06)

Traits of a Healthy Spirituality

This book is a great motivator for those developing their spiritual life. In an engaging style it defines and describes twenty indicators of a healthy spirituality such as self-esteem, joy, and commitment.

144 pages, $9.95 (order M-87)

Jesus, I'm a Teacher, Too
Guidance and Inspiration from the Gospels

Whether used for personal or group reflection and prayer, this book will help religion teachers learn from St. Mark's Gospel what it means to be a dedicated teacher. The author reveals the compassion and gifts of Jesus, the master teacher. Insights and inspiration abound. Great gift book for catechists.

144 pp, $9.95 (order M-33)

Available at religious bookstores or from:

TWENTY-THIRD PUBLICATIONS

P.O. BOX 180 • 185 WILLOW ST. • MYSTIC, CT 06355 • 1-860-536-2611 • 1-800-321-0411 • FAX 1-800-572-0788

Call for a free catalog